THE CRITICAL YEARS:
AMERICAN FOREIGN POLICY
1793–1823

PROBLEMS IN AMERICAN HISTORY

EDITOR

LOREN BARITZ

State University of New York, Albany

THE LEADERSHIP OF ABRAHAM LINCOLN
Don E. Fehrenbacher

THE AMERICAN CONSTITUTION
Paul Goodman

THE AMERICAN REVOLUTION
Richard J. Hooker

AMERICA IN THE COLD WAR
Walter LaFeber

THE ORIGINS OF THE COLD WAR, 1941–1947
Walter LaFeber

AMERICAN IMPERIALISM IN 1898
Richard H. Miller

TENSIONS IN AMERICAN PURITANISM
Richard Reinitz

THE GREAT AWAKENING
Darrett B. Rutman

WORLD WAR I AT HOME
David F. Trask

THE CRITICAL YEARS, AMERICAN FOREIGN POLICY, 1793–1825
Patrick C. T. White

THE CRITICAL YEARS: AMERICAN FOREIGN POLICY

1793–1823

EDITED BY

Patrick C. T. White
University of Toronto

John Wiley & Sons, Inc.
New York · London · Sydney · Toronto

Library of Congress Catalogue Card Number: 78-126232

Cloth: ISBN 0-471-94070-4   Paper: ISBN 0-471-94071-2
Printed in the United States of America

10 9 8 7 6 5 4 3 2 1

SERIES PREFACE

This series is an introduction to the most important problems in the writing and study of American history. Some of these problems have been the subject of debate and argument for a long time, although others only recently have been recognized as controversial. However, in every case, the student will find a vital topic, an understanding of which will deepen his knowledge of social change in America.

The scholars who introduce and edit the books in this series are teaching historians who have written history in the same general area as their individual books. Many of them are leading scholars in their fields, and all have done important work in the collective search for better historical understanding.

Because of the talent and the specialized knowledge of the individual editors, a rigid editorial format has not been imposed on them. For example, some of the editors believe that primary source material is necessary to their subjects. Some believe that their material should be arranged to show conflicting interpretations. Others have decided to use the selected materials as evidence for their own interpretations. The individual editors have been given the freedom to handle their books in the way that their own experience and knowledge indicate is best. The overall result is a series built up from the individual decisions of working scholars in the various fields, rather than one that conforms to a uniform editorial decision.

A common goal (rather than a shared technique) is the bridge of this series. There is always the desire to bring the reader as close to these problems as possible. One result of this objective is an emphasis of the nature and consequences of problems and events, with a de-emphasis of the more purely historiographical issues. The goal is to involve the student in the reality of crisis, the inevitability of ambiguity, and the excitement of finding a way through the historical maze.

Above all, this series is designed to show students how experienced historians read and reason. Although health is not contagious, intellectual engagement may be. If we show students something significant in a phrase or a passage that they otherwise may have missed, we will have accomplished part of our objective. When students see something that passed us by, then the process will have been made whole. This active and mutual involvement of editor and reader with a significant human problem will rescue the study of history from the smell and feel of dust.

Loren Baritz

INTRODUCTION

My main purpose, Washington said in 1793, is to "keep our people in peace." He and his successors were to find, however, that achieving this desirable goal was a delicate, difficult, and even impossible task. For despite all the energy and skill which various chief executives exercised, events in Europe over which the United States had little or no control swept America into a war which all had striven to avoid.

Washington recognized, at once, that the outbreak of a war in Europe between Britain and France in 1793 posed a grave threat to the United States. There were those who felt that America was bound, through both treaty and friendship, to come to the aid of France. But the President, who did not allow emotion to overrule reason, rejected this view, and in April 1793 issued a proclamation of neutrality. But proclaiming neutrality and preserving it were two different matters. To achieve the latter required all the President's considerable skill and foresight. In 1794 a partial settlement was reached with Britain through Jay's Treaty which provided for the withdrawal of her troops from the northwest posts and created mixed commissions to resolve certain boundary disputes with British North America. The treaty was harshly denounced by those who argued that a solution to maritime disputes should also have been secured. But Britain was not likely to surrender to a neutral United States practices which she deemed vital to her survival. Because of Washington's experience with dangers from abroad and fractions at home, he decided to issue a farewell address in which he warned that permanent foreign alliances and partisan domestic strife would ill serve the nation. He did not suggest absolute neutrality for he knew that it was as unattainable as it was undesirable.

The years immediately following Washington's departure from office proved the wisdom of his prescription and the difficulty of following it. The flagrant violation of American rights by France led to what contemporaries called a "quasi-war" with that nation. At times, indeed, it appeared that many Federalists, including the President, would have welcomed a formal declaration of hostilities against her. But Adam tempered his behavior and his language and finally secured in 1800 a settlement of the issues in dispute. His actions bore additional fruit in 1803 when Jefferson was able to purchase the Louisiana territories. In a single stroke he secured for the United States an enormous expanse of the continent, added greatly to the power of the nation, and gave to all Americans a renewed sense of strength and destiny.

All these were soon to be needed, for the war between Britain and France broke out again with renewed intensity in 1803 and placed unprecedented stresses and strains on the United States. The war at sea was the immediate cause of America's distress. Great Britain had promptly renewed impressment—a practice which struck at the very heart of the United States. The nature of the challenge here was twofold. First, native-born Americans were often seized by officers of the Royal Navy in order to fill out crews depleted by desertion or battle. Second, the law officers of the crown argued that native-born Englishmen could be called on to serve the nation in times of great peril. This service could not be evaded by claiming that one had become a naturalized American, for Britain did not recognize the legitimacy of this new and novel practice. She clung, instead, to the doctrine of "indefeasable nationality," by which she meant that citizenship bestowed by birth could never be altered. As a consequence, Englishmen who had become American citizens were forcibly removed from ships on the high seas. In addition, of course, Britain reserved the right to capture deserters. And these existed in embarrassingly large numbers, since the harsh and unrelenting conditions of service in the Royal Navy compared unfavorably with the high wages and attractive living conditions generally typical of the American merchant marine.

Besides impressment, the United States felt injured by a variety of other British practices. First, there was the "Rule of 1756" which arbitrarily stated that a nation could not trade during war with a country whose commerce had been closed to it in times of peace. This measure was specifically aimed at American trade with the French West Indies—a trade which France encouraged after her ships had been swept from the high seas by the Royal Navy. Second, there was the matter of blockades. The United States held to the traditional view that only a specific point could be blockaded and that such a blockade was legal only if it were enforced by an ever-present fleet of ships. Britain, however, argued that she could blockade whole stretches of coastline and that it could be legally enforced by vessels cruising offshore. Third, the United States defined contraband as arms and accoutrements of war, but Britain insisted that it included foodstuffs as well. Fourth, there was the argument over broken and continuous voyages. A broken voyage was one in which an American vessel took goods from a foreign port to the United States, where the commodities were landed and duties paid on them before re-export. A continuous voyage was one in which American ships merely touched the United States in the second stage of its trip. Britain stated that if the voyage were truly broken the goods in question became American and were, therefore, not subject to seizure. But the United States insisted that the British definition of a broken voyage was too narrowly legalistic and restrictive. And finally, there were the Orders in Council. These far-ranging and damaging British decrees prohibited all commerce between ports under Napoleon's control and extended the blockade to every area which, by order of France, excluded British goods. It is quite true, of course, that France's Berlin and Milan decrees, as well as the capricious behavior of her officers in her ports, inflicted severe penalties on America. But since Britain controlled the high seas, particularly after Trafalgar, her actions were more menacing and damaging. To resolve all these disputes would have taken a degree of patience, wisdom, and good fortune that providence seldom bestows on men. Certainly, Jefferson threw all his generous talents into the battle. But ability and dedication were finally no substitutes for power and position. And try as the President might, through embargoes, economic sanctions, reason, and persuasion, he was destined to fail.

James Madison, his successor, fared no better. A man of lesser stature and narrower intellect, it fell to him to make the unhappy decision that, since negotiation and coercion had failed, force was all that remained. It was a decision that he arrived at reluctantly and only after great pressure had been exerted on him by those in Congress who had tired of endless talk and fruitless discussion. His war message was happily received by many, but violently opposed by some. Federalists still felt that Britain was the last bastion of ordered government and freedom and should not be attacked; they argued that negotiations were still possible and insisted that republican institutions were too untested and fragile to stand the shock of war. But others urged that the Republic could not survive if it did not defend its interests and that national honor and America's sovereignty demanded war.

If those involved in making the declaration of war were in sharp disagreement, it is little wonder that succeeding generations have offered different views of what brought on, in Calhoun's words, "America's second war of independence." Explanations of this conflict range from one end of the spectrum to the other. There are some who see it as arising from a desire to annex the fertile land of Canada or to suppress an Indian menace there which threatened the security of the western frontier. There are others who feel it came as a result of the British Orders in Council, or party division, or a desire to protect American honor and sovereignty. The latter arguments are, on balance, more persuasive than the former. But because the nation went into war in a fractious spirit and with a divided Congress, the disputes over causation will continue.

Those who had supported the declaration were convinced that the war would be swiftly fought and easily won. They were wrong, as so often are those who think that war is a simple business. The conquest of Canada was not, as even Jefferson thought it would be, a mere matter of marching. Its occupation was to prove impossible and the fighting along its borders was frequently bloody and indecisive. But if the United States could not win, neither could Britain. She might control the high seas, but an invasion of the United States was a different matter. Even with the use of enormous forces, its outcome would be doubtful.

And so both sides sought peace. It took hard bargaining to bring about and required both parties to moderate demands that were first based on illusion rather than reality. The peace that was achieved reflected the world as it was, for it simply called for a return to the *status quo ante bellum.* This did not mean that the United States gained nothing from years of war. She proved to the world that she would fight for her interests and she showed that her republican institutions were sturdier and more resilient than many had thought. And, as Gallatin observed, she renewed her sense of nationalism and purpose. Finally, she was given a glimpse of the danger of sectionalism and the hazards of disunity. Those opponents of the war who talked of New England's secession gave proof of the perils that could engulf a nation whose• people were divided over the purposes of the national government.

The Treaty of Ghent ended the war of 1812, but it did not resolve all Anglo-American differences. The question of American access to fisheries in British North American waters and the problem of the boundary west of the Lake of the Woods still remained. The British argued that fishing liberties granted in 1783 had been abrogated by the war and insisted that the boundary should provide for Britain's free navigation of the Mississippi River. In 1818 a convention was negotiated which settled both these contentious issues. The Americans were given the "liberty" to fish along specified sections of the coasts of Newfoundland and Labrador as well as the shores of the Magdalen Islands. They were also granted the "liberty" to land and dry fish on the unsettled shores of portions of the maritime provinces. The boundary west of the Lake of the Woods was drawn along the 49° to the "Stony Mountains." Beyond the Rocky Mountains, of course, lay Oregon, and it was agreed that both powers should have free and equal access to it. The "joint occupation" of that territory, therefore, began in 1818.

The resolution of border problems in the North was matched by an equally favorable settlement in the South. The United States had long been deeply concerned by the Spanish possession of the Floridas. As early as 1810 America had occupied a portion of West Florida and in 1812 Congress had passed a bill secretly authorizing the President to take control of East Florida. But at the war's end that territory still lay in Spanish hands. It was quite clear, however, that most Americans viewed the annexation of Florida as a desirable national goal. It was also quite clear that Spain's weakness was such that she could not retain Florida unless some European power gave her assistance. And Castlereagh, the British Foreign Secretary, made it perfectly plain that such help would not be forthcoming from his government. The result was the Adams-Onis Treaty of 1819 which ceded the Floridas to the United States. It was a diplomatic victory of the first magnitude because, by it, America ran her borders west to the Red River and then north to the Arkansas River. From the source of this river the line was to go to the 42° and then due west to the Pacific. America now stretched from sea to sea.

The disintegration of Spain's dominion in the New World posed still further problems. The end of the war in Europe had seen the restoration of the "legitimate" monarchy in Spain and a restoration of her authority in her overseas possessions. In 1817, however, rebellion broke out in her American colonies once more and raised the spectre of European intervention in the affairs of the Western hemisphere. In particular, Britain was concerned over the possibility that France might help Spain reassert her authority over her unruly possessions. George Canning, the British Foreign Secretary, proposed to Richard Rush, the American minister in London, that their two governments had a mutual interest in seeing that the Spanish colonies did not fall into the hands of other European powers. His suggestion was received with sympathy and warmth, but John Quincy Adams' deep distrust of Canning led him to urge on President Monroe a unilateral American declaration of policy and intent. And so the Monroe Doctrine was born.

The United States had come a long way in forty years. She had undertaken successful negotiations with European nations and she had fought a war with Great Britain. She had extended her boundaries from the Atlantic to the Pacific and she had warned others that the Western hemisphere was no longer to be interfered with. The United States was, by 1823, no mean power.

CONTENTS

PART III

Peace and the Postwar Settlement   113

PART IV

Suggested Further Reading   163

THE CRITICAL YEARS:
AMERICAN FOREIGN POLICY
1793–1823

PART ONE

The Challenge of Neutrality

1 FROM   *John C. Miller*
The Federalist Era

The outbreak of the French Revolution in 1793 was widely welcomed in the United States, since most Americans saw it as the overthrowing of a corrupt and tyrannical regime. Few realized that it would lead to a general European conflict that would imperil the security of the United States. When Britain and France went to war in 1793, the United States was faced with a political dilemma. The Franco-American Alliance of 1778 raised the question of whether the United States should come to the aid of France. Some argued that since the latter had supported America during her Revolution, simple decency called for a reciprocal gesture of equal magnitude.

But foreign policy should not be made on the basis of sentiment, and President Washington and his cabinet were not going to allow themselves to be stampeded into taking actions that could jeopardize the security of their country. They asked themselves whether the Alliance of 1778 clearly called for an American military commitment. A reading of the treaty showed that only if Britain invaded the French West Indies could the United States be called on for aid. Furthermore, France never pressed the United States for support because she was happy to have her as a neutral supplier of goods. In any event, Washington issued a Proclamation of Neutrality enjoining American citizens to be "friendly and impartial toward the belligerent powers." The following extract by Professor John C. Miller is from the Federalist Era *and elaborates on America's dilemma in this difficult period.*

SOURCE. John C. Miller, *The Federalist Era*, pp. 128–132 Copyright © 1960 by John C. Miller. Reprinted by permission of Harper & Row, Publishers, Inc., and the author.

THE NEUTRALITY PROCLAMATION, 1793

The French Revolution became the paramount issue in American politics when, early in 1793, France proclaimed itself a republic, declared war upon Great Britain, and appointed Citizen Edmond Genêt minister to the United States. By abolishing the monarchy, France joined the ideological camp of the United States; by going to war with Great Britain, it raised the question of American aid under the Treaty of Alliance of 1778; and by sending Genêt to the United States, it precipitated a crisis in Franco-American relations.

Both Hamilton and Jefferson wished to preserve the neutrality of the United States, but they differed markedly as to how this objective could be best achieved. Hamilton argued that the treaties of commerce and alliance, which dated from 1778 and by the terms of which the United States guaranteed France in possession of its West Indian islands and opened its ports to French privateers, should be declared "temporarily and provisionally suspended." While the Secretary of the Treasury admitted that treaties between nations remained in force regardless of changes in the form of government of either signatory, he insisted that this rule applied "only in reference to a *change*, which has been finally *established* and secured." It did not apply, he asserted, when, as in the present case, such a change was "pending and in contest and which may never be consummated." He also contended that the United States was under no obligation to defend the French West Indies, because such action would expose the nation "to a *great extremity* of danger." The treaty with France specified American aid only in case of a defensive war; and Hamilton took full advantage of the fact that France had declared war upon Great Britain in January, 1793. As for Citizen Genêt, Hamilton strenuously opposed his reception by the United States government—to receive Genêt, he said, was to recognize the French republic and the binding force of the Franco-American treaties.

Jefferson was horrified by the cavalier attitude assumed by Hamilton toward the treaty obligations of the United States. In the cabinet meetings held early in April 1793, the Secretary of State took the position that the Franco-American treaties were compacts between peoples, not merely between governments. The question of the defense of the West Indies and the danger it entailed of war with Great Britain might be safely left, he said, to the future; nor was it the present duty of the United States to decide whether France was engaged in defensive or offensive war. And, finally, Jefferson insisted that Genêt be received as the representative of the duly constituted government of France.

Nor were the two cabinet officers agreed upon the question how the United States ought to acquaint the world with its intention of remaining neutral in the European war. Hamilton's reading of the Constitution left no doubt in his mind that the President possessed the power in the absence of Congress to proclaim and enforce "the neutrality of the nation." From that document, however, Jefferson drew the opposite conclusion: since the warmaking power was vested in Congress, he inclined to the view that only Congress could properly commit the country to neutrality. Moreover, whereas Hamilton favored an immediate declaration of neutrality, Jefferson wished to delay action in the hope that the belligerents would make concessions to the commerce of the United States and other non-belligerents in order to ensure their neutrality. In short, he proposed to put a price tag upon the neutrality of the United States.

In the cabinet discussion, Hamilton lost on two of the points in controversy: President Washington decided not to declare the treaties suspended and he decided to receive Citizen Genêt, thereby making the United States the first nation to accept an emissary from the French Republic. In the matter of the competence of the Chief Executive to issue a proclamation of neutrality, however, the President adopted Hamilton's views. Disclaiming any suggestion that he could bind Congress and asserting that "his main view was to keep our people in peace," Washington nonetheless resolved to meet the crisis by an epoch-making exercise of presidential authority, calculated to make the President a greater power than even George III in the formulation and conduct of foreign policy. The elimination of the word "neutrality" from the proclamation removed Jefferson's objection, although not his doubts and mis-givings, and on April 19, 1793, the cabinet unanimously recom-mended that the President save the peace by issuing in the name of the government of the United States a proclamation of "neutrality."

The President's proclamation gave assurance to foreign nations that the United States intended to pursue "a conduct friendly and impartial towards the belligerent powers." To that end, it pro-hibited American citizens from "aiding or abetting hostilities" or otherwise engaging in unneutral acts within the jurisdiction of the United States.

While Republicans were content that the United States should remain neutral, they hotly resented the use of the word "impartial" and the constraints placed upon their freedom of action by the President. Had Washington forgotten, they asked, that France was "under God, the saviour of America," and that upon the continued friendship of France "the future glory, honor, welfare, commerce, agriculture and manufactures of *America* essentially depend?" Hugh Brackenridge, a Republican leader of western Pennsylvania, summed up the attitude of his party when he declared that "the cause of France is the cause of man, and neutrality is desertion." What these citizens wanted was to enjoy all the immunities of neutrality and still exercise the privilege of aiding France against the "Despots of Europe." They thought solely in terms of American rights; when President Washington reminded them of their duties, they raised the cry that he was acting unconstitutionally.

Wary of attacking the President directly, Republicans attributed his dereliction to his "evil counsellors," the chief of whom, of course, being Alexander Hamilton. The Secretary of the Treasury gave credence to this suspicion that he was responsible for the neutrality proclamation by the ardor with which he defended it in the newspapers. Under the pseudonym of "Pacificus" Hamilton published a series of articles purporting to show that the President was within his constitutional rights; that the proclamation was binding upon the nation; that war upon the side of France would be an unmitigated disaster for the United States; and that France was and always had been—even when aiding the United States during the War of Independence—actuated by self-interest.

Fearful that these doctrines would warp the government into monarchism, Jefferson appealed to his friend James Madison: "For God's sake, my dear Sir, take up your pen, select the most striking heresies, and cut him to pieces in the face of the public." Taking the name "Helvidius," Madison set forth the true "republican" canons: Congress controls foreign policy; the powers of the President in the diplomatic field are instrumental only; the executive department is more prone to war than is the legislature—"war is, in fact, the true source of executive aggrandizement"—and the proclamation of neutrality was a unilateral interpretation of the Franco-American treaties and enjoined an impartiality that was irreconcilable with Americans' moral obligations. Madison advocated neutrality, but he insisted that it be proclaimed by Congress. The former exponent of excutive powers was now bent upon whittling the Chief Magistrate down to a stature considerably smaller than that of Congress.

2 FROM *Paul A. Varg*
Foreign Policies of the Founding Fathers

The proclamation of Neutrality saved the United States from immediate involvement in the war in Europe, but it did not remove her from all the dangers which that conflict created. The United States was, of course, in a particularly delicate position for she was not only faced with complicated maritime problems, but she was also grappling with still unresolved disputes arising from the Treaty of 1783.

The maritime issues proved in the long run to be more difficult of resolution. The United States, as a neutral, wished to be able to trade freely with Europe and the West Indies; she wanted to have her seamen free from impressment and her ships immune to illegal search and seizure. Furthermore, she disputed the novel interpretations of certain maritime practices pertaining to contraband and blockades which Britain was advancing. Beyond these were the differences over the boundary in the northeast and the persistent retention by Britain of the northwest posts.

These were challenging difficulties to resolve. And if Britain proved to be intransigent on some issues, what weapons or pressures could America use to gain her ends? Jay accepted less than a perfect treaty rather than jeopardize a settlement. His actions were fiercely disputed then and are still questioned now. Could he have secured better terms? Was Britain so vulnerable that she would have met America's demands in order to maintain her friendship? What role did Hamilton play in the negotiations? These are questions and issues which Dean Paul A. Varg addresses himself to in this extract from his study of the period.

JAY'S TREATY, 1794

The debate over relations with Great Britain became inextricably involved with the question of which of the two emerging parties was to control the federal government for the next four years. The Jay Treaty was a reasonable give-and-take compromise of the issues between the two countries. What rendered it so assailable was not the compromise spelled out between the two nations but the fact

SOURCE. Paul A. Varg, *Foreign Policies of the Founding Fathers* (East Lansing: Michigan State University Press, 1963), pp. 95–114. Reprinted by permission of the publisher.

that it was not a compromise between the two political parties at home. Embodying the views of the Federalists, the treaty repudiated the foreign policy of the opposing party. The Anti-Federalists saw in their party's foreign policy a set of principles of fundamental importance not only in relation to the outside world but also basic to the very nature of society they were seeking to establish at home. They were likewise intent on taking control of the government in the approaching election. Tied to the question of the ratification of the treaty was the question of the future prospects of the two camps of political leaders.

The British expected their rivals to fight. If they didn't, observed Henry Adams, they looked upon them as cowardly or mean. Alexander Hamilton's determination not to offend Great Britain invited a high handed and callous disregard that nettled the American agrarians. The United States had turned its breeches to receive British kicks. So it seemed to Jefferson.

The list of grievances against Great Britain included retention of the military posts in the Northwest, at least indirect encouragement to the Indians who had launched a costly and troublesome war, the carrying away of several thousand Negro slaves at the close of the Revolution without making compensation, and a policy of extorting the most out of American trade without offering reciprocal advantages. For two years Jefferson invited negotiation of the issues without gaining any response. To this frustrating experience George Hammond, the British minister, added a tone of conversation that convinced Jefferson and Madison that the British planned to make war. A speech by Lord Dorchester, Governor General of Canada, encouraging the Indians to make war, and the building of a new fort at Maumee by Governor Simcoe, strengthened this view.

The British game poorly prepared the way for American acceptance of British rulings as to commerce on the high seas upon the outbreak of hostilities between Great Britain and France in February 1793. On June 8 Lord Grenville issued orders to naval commanders to seize all ships carrying corn, flour, or meal bound for a port in France or any port controlled by the armies of France. Hammond, the British minister, defended the order with the dubious assertion that the law of nations sanctioned the treatment of all provisions as contraband and subject to confiscation "where the depriving an enemy of these supplies, is one of the means intended to be employed for reducing him to reasonable terms of peace." Jefferson jumped upon the British contention with the eagerness of one who believed that the prospective enemy had over-reached himself. In an instruction to Thomas Pinckney, American minister in London, Jefferson damned the measure as "so manifestly contrary to the law of nations, that nothing more would seem necessary, than to observe that it is so."

Jefferson carefully outlines the dangerous implications of the British contention for the United States. "We see, then, a practice begun, to which no time, no circumstances, prescribe any limits, and which strikes at the root of our agriculture, that branch of industry which gives food, clothing and comfort, to the great mass of inhabitants of these States," he stated. "If any nation whatever has a right," he said, "to shut up, to our produce, all the ports of the earth, except her own, and those of her friends, she may shut up these also, and confine us within our limits." "No nation," he proclaimed, "can subscribe to such pretensions; no nation can agree, at the mere will or interest of another, to have its peaceable industry suspended, and its citizens reduced to idleness and want."

The question likewise involved, said Jefferson, the right of the American government to defend itself against involuntary involvement in war. To put the United States into a position in which it furnished supplies to one belligerent and not to the other could only be deemed a cause for war by the latter. There was no difference, he explained, in the United States restraining commerce with France and her suffering Great Britain to prohibit it. France would consider the latter a mere pretext. To permit Great Britain to bar commerce with France would impose on the United States a neutral duty to likewise withhold supplies from Great Britain. "This is a dilemma," he said, "which Great Britain has no right to force upon us, and for which no pretext can be found in any part of our conduct."

Jefferson's firm posture contrasted with the note of supplication that so characterized Hamilton's every intrusion into foreign affairs when these involved Great Britain. Jefferson and Madison meant to demand respect. Privately, Jefferson confessed to Madison that he had no hope of Great Britain revoking her measures. These two architects of the republic aimed at impressing the British with the fact that they could not deal with the United States with impunity.

Jefferson's efforts to counteract the appeasement policy of Hamilton gained strength when the British, in September, 1794, negotiated a truce between Portugal and the Algerines without the express consent of Portugal and on terms unsatisfactory to the Portuguese. Immediately the Algerines sailed into the Atlantic and began to attack American shipping, a result that Edward Church, American consul at Lisbon, described as the primary aim of the British in negotiating the truce. Church wrote to the Secretary of State that the truce furnished further evidence that British "envy, jealousy, and hatred, will never be appeased, and that they will leave nothing unattempted to effect our ruin." In the next few months Americans denounced the British move as a deliberate act of hostility.

The rising feeling against Great Britain furnished the backdrop for Jefferson's report in December to the House of Representatives on the condition of American commerce. The Secretary of State again assumed a posture of forthrightness. Three facts in the report, duly emphasized, called for legislative measures. First, while imports from Great Britain totalled $15,285,428 compared to $2,068,348 from France, American vessels carried 116,410 tons from France and only 43,580 tons from Great Britain. Secondly, a greater part of the exports to Great Britain were re-exported "under the useless charges of an intermediate deposite, and double voyage." One-third of the indigo, four-fifths of the tobacco and rice, and, when prices were normal, all of the grain, were re-exported. Thirdly, Jefferson pointed to the exclusion of American ships from the British West Indies and the prohibition against both vessels and produce in the British continental colonies and Newfoundland. Jefferson called for remedies. "Free commerce and navigation," he said, "are not to be given in exchange for restrictions and vexations, nor are they likely to produce a relaxation of them."

The evil could not be measured solely in economic terms. Jefferson warned: "But it is a resource of defense, that our navigation will admit neither neglect nor forbearance." On their seaboard, he observed, Americans are open to injury and have a commerce to be protected. This security could only be achieved "by possessing a respectable body of citizen-seamen, and of artists and establishments in readiness for ship-building." To rectify the grievances, argued Jefferson, the United States should introduce discriminations against the offending nation.

On January 3, 1794, the House of Representatives took up the report and James Madison introduced a set of resolutions for carrying out Jefferson's program. One of the most crucial debates in the entire history of American foreign policy ensued. Madison explained euphemistically that what "we receive from other nations are but luxuries to us, which, if we choose to throw aside, we could deprive part of the manufacturers of those luxuries, of even bread, if we are forced to the contest of self-denial." Great Britain must be forced into a more equitable relationship. "She refuses not only our manufactures," he stressed, "but the articles we wish most to send her—our wheat and flour, our fish, and our salted provisions. These constitute our best staples for exportation, as her manufactures constitute hers."

Madison expanded on the evils from Great Britain's great predominance. A sudden derangement of commerce could be brought about by the caprice of the British sovereigns. The situation subjected the United States to the danger of suffering a serious shock should bankruptcy overtake England. England's numerous wars meant that dependence on her would result in serious embarrassments. Finally, Madison spoke of the influence "that may be conveyed in public councils by a nation directing the course of our trade by her capital, and holding so great a share in our pecuniary institutions, and the effect that may finally ensue in our taste, our manners, and our form of Government itself."

Two Virginia representatives bore the brunt of the burden of defending Madison's program. John Nicholas affirmed that the nation's interest demanded a larger share of the carrying trade. He made light of British credit. It only served, he said, to lead farmers into debt. As to the danger of a decline in revenue from import duties if Great Britain retaliated, Nicholas contended that the revenue could be made up by other taxes.

William B. Giles appealed to patriotism. He wished to know why there was not the same willingness to oppose Britain as at the time of the Revolution. To those who counselled patience, Giles replied that "patience is an admirable beast of burden." "Instead, therefore, of patience and forbearance," Giles explained, "wisdom, caution herself, would prescribe boldness, enterprise, energy, firmness."

"Madison's wild system" struck terror in the hearts of the stolid representatives of business. Why imperil the nation's growth and prosperity? William Smith of South Carolina, armed with a speech prepared by Hamilton, argued that England pursued at least as generous a policy as other nations. He saw no reason to grieve over the predominance of British imports. That dominance flowed from natural causes, the availability of British credit, the influence of long habit, and the advantage of trading in the British market that offered such a great variety of goods. He stressed the need for foreign capital: "There is no country in the world in a situation to benefit so much by the aid of foreign capital, as the United States." "This arises," said this spokesman for Hamilton, "not only from the inadequateness, compared with the objects of employment of our own capital, but from the condition in which we are, with numerous resources unexplored and undeveloped."

Fisher Ames charged Madison with wishing to substitute an improbable theory for an actual prosperity. And the outcome of that theory, if applied, would drive Great Britain into a system of retaliation. Great Britain, he warned, could only consider discrimination at the present critical juncture of world affairs as an unneutral act.

Ames knew that the present state of hostility toward Great Britain brought support to Madison's measures on patriotic grounds. He sought to undermine their patriotic appeal with the assertion that if "our trade is already on a profitable footing, it is on a respectable one." "While they will smoke our tobacco, and eat our provisions," said Ames, "it is very immaterial, both to the consumer and the producer, what are the politics of the two countries, excepting so far as their quarrels may disturb the benefits of their mutual intercourse."

The debate came to a close one month after it had begun. On February 5 the House voted to delay action until the first Monday in March. Madison agreed to the postponement because he found it awkward to do otherwise.

The renewal of the debate in March took place in a setting where the most ardent of British friends deplored her policies. On November 6, 1793, the British Crown ordered the seizure of all ships laden with goods, the produce of any colony belonging to France, or carrying provisions or other supplies for the use of French colonies. By early March the British held 250 American vessels in their possession in the West Indies alone and American captains found that numerous obstacles in the form of legal procedures barred the way to the British promise of compensation. Even Theodore Sedgwick, long a supporter of appeasement of the British, confided:

"Such indeed are the injuries which we have received from Great Britain that I believe I should not hesitate on going to war, but that we must in that case be allied to France, which would be an alliance with principles which would prostitute liberty & destroy every species of security."

The central issue now changed from that of Madison's resolutions to the best way of gaining immediate relief. Madison's measures had been framed as a long term program for bringing a better balance into foreign relations. Now the situation had become so critical that Madison acknowledged that commercial measures were "not the precise remedy to be pressed in first order; but they are in every view & argument proper to make part of our standing laws till the principles of reciprocity be established by mutual arrangements." The real question now centered on what measures would be most likely to promote a successful negotiation.

Theodore Sedgwick took the lead in calling for a program of defense that included a standing army. He soon discovered that the advocates of Madison's proposals opposed every such defense measure. He wrote to his friend Ephraim Williams: "Is it not strange that at the moment these madmen are doing every thing in their power to irritate G.B. they are opposing every attempt to put our country in a posture of defense." The grounds of opposition to Sedgwick's defense measures lay in fear of a standing army that would be at the beck and call of the executive for purposes other than defense against foreign aggression. Madison suspected that the emphasis on defense had its origin in part in an effort to sidetrack his commercial proposals but that the main aim lay elsewhere. He wrote to Jefferson: "you understand the game behind the curtain too well to perceive the old trick of turning every contingency into a resource for accumulating force in the government."

The agrarians preferred resolutions and economic weapons, but Madison's resolutions soon fell by the wayside as more extreme measures came forward. On March 26 the House, sitting as a committee of the whole, passed a resolution in favor of granting the President the power to lay an embargo for thirty days. A month later Congress laid an embargo on all foreign shipping for one month. Congress renewed the measure for another thirty days in April.

"Such madness, my friend, such madness! and yet many good men voted for it . . . ," wrote Sedgwick. A few weeks earlier Sedgwick had called for the defeat of "Madison's wild system" so that the country could prepare for defense. Such measures, argued the followers of Hamilton, would improve the position of the United

States in negotiating. The opponents' proposals, Sedgwick believed, would "enlist her pride and insolence against us."

Late in March Jonathan Dayton, of New Jersey, introduced a resolution calling for the sequestration of all debts due from the citizens of the United States to subjects of Great Britain. William Giles supported the measure with the contention that only if the British people were brought to fear for their own interests would they exert pressure on their government to negotiate. Dayton's resolution failed to pass.

In April the battle raged on another front. President Washington appointed John Jay special envoy to Great Britain. No appointment would have proved popular with the Republicans who much preferred to take economic measures before entering upon negotiations. The naming of Jay convinced them that further appeasement was to be expected. Jay had been ready to agree to the closing of the Mississippi in 1786 in return for a commercial treaty with Spain. His critics predicted that he would yield to the merchants again and negotiate a treaty that sacrificed the true national interest. The Republican societies engaged at once in a campaign of vilification of the envoy. This did not deter the Senate, always on the side of the executive branch, from confirming the appointment.

The instructions carefully spelled out the grievances, spoliations, violations of the peace treaty, and the restrictions on trade. No commercial treaty should be negotiated unless American ships gained the right to enter the British West Indies. But the firm tone of the instructions did not obscure the fact that the governing group at home desperately needed some kind of a treaty that would put an end to the dangerous tendency to take hostile measures toward England. Jay thought as did Hamilton and the merchants, and one paragraph of his instructions undoubtedly carried a special significance to him. That paragraph read: "You will mention, with due stress, the general irritation of the United States at the vexations, spoliations, captures, &c. And being on the field of negotiation you will be more able to judge, than can be prescribed now, how far you may state the difficulty which may occur in restraining the violence of some of our exasperated citizens." And besides his formal instructions Jay carried with him the letters from Hamilton urging a settlement and outlining its nature.

Jay found Lord Grenville congenial and the British population amiable. His reports made clear at once that Great Britain desired peace. The triumphs of France at that time made any thought of engaging a new enemy most unpalatable. The British offered no resistance to an agreement to evacuate the posts in the Northwest. They yielded to Jay's interpretation of the peace treaty on the two major boundary disputes and agreed to have them settled by commission.

Jay looked to Hamilton rather than to Secretary of State Edmund Randolph. Hamilton fathered the negotiations, arranged the appointment of Jay, and watched over the whole proceeding with a paternal eye. The Madison proposals, the Dayton motion for the sequestration of debts, and the Non-Importation Act portended war and Hamilton saw in a new treaty with Great Britain the one way to put out the fire that the agrarians were kindling. He wrote to Jay, "We are both impressed equally strongly with the great importance of a right adjustment of all matters of past controversy and future good understanding with Great Britain." But he recognized with perspicacity that any surrender of legitimate interests or too great a bending to British wishes would invite a revulsion among the American people that would make amicable relations impossible. Hamilton warned, "it will be better to do nothing, than to do any thing that will not stand the test of the severest scrutiny—and especially, which may be construed into the relinquishment of a substantial right or interest."

Hamilton's letters penetrated more deeply into the problems of the negotiation than did the formal instructions. He foresaw that the most troublesome point in the discussions would be that of the seizures of American ships. It would be difficult and in fact impossible for Great Britain to accept the American interpretation of what constituted contraband or to yield the policy of seizing produce on its way to French ports. The Americans would find an agreement to accede to British practice equally unsavory. Hamilton did not hesitate to describe the British order of November 6 as atrocious.

Hamilton's approach to this delicate problem lay in placing the unpalatable British measures between two layers of extremely pleasing concessions. He wrote to Jay: "If you can effect solid arrangements with regard to the points unexecuted of the treaty of peace, the question of indemnification may be managed with less rigor, and may be still more laxly dealt with, if a truly beneficial treaty of commerce, embracing privileges in the West India Islands, can be established." Hamilton wished to push the British as far as possible on indemnification; it would serve no purpose to "make any arrangement on the *mere appearance* of indemnification." If the British would not agree to a firm guarantee, thought Hamilton, then it would be best to leave the United States free to act in whatever manner might be deemed proper.

In July Lord Grenville gave to Jay a draft of the proposed treaty altering the one submitted by Jay a few days earlier. Grenville's project probably reached Philadelphia in late August. Hamilton examined it and found two major weaknesses. He took strong exception to placing British vessels in American ports on the same basis as American vessels. He objected to Article XII dealing with the right of American vessels to enter the ports of the West Indies because the privilege was limited to two years and because it would have prohibited Americans from transporting produce of any of the West Indies to any other part of the world than the United States.

Edmund Randolph, Jefferson's successor as Secretary of State, scrutinized Grenville's draft with an equally critical eye. The refusal of the British to make compensation for the slaves taken at the close of the Revolution disturbed him more than any other aspect. He too considered Article XII unsatisfactory. He likewise objected to postponing British evacuation of the Northwest posts until June 1796.

The criticisms of Hamilton and Randolph did not reach Jay until the treaty had been signed. Jay held that the treaty represented the utmost that could be expected in dealing with a nation so proud and so powerful. The fact that Article XII contained a two year limitation and prohibited the United States from engaging in the all important carrying trade from the West Indies struck Jay as less important than the fact that a wedge had been driven into the British barrier against American vessels.

The essence of Jay's defense of the treaty lay in his explanation to Edmund Randolph. "Perhaps it is not very much to be regretted that all our differences are merged in this treaty, without having been decided; disagreeable imputations are thereby avoided, and the door of conciliation is fairly and widely opened, by the *essential* justice done, and the conveniences granted to each other by the parties," he reflected. The treaty removed the most serious apprehensions concerning British intentions in the West. The two boundary disputes in the Northwest and the Northeast were to be settled by commissions. A *modus vivendi* assuring Americans of compensation for the losses on the high seas removed some of the ignitive quality from the controversy over neutral rights. The Hamiltonians, anxious about what war would do to the fiscal system and dreading a war in which they would inevitably become the allies of France considered these two as the great gains of the treaty.

The final treaty arrived in Philadelphia on March 7, 1795. Washington and Randolph decided at once not to make it public. The Senate received it in June and approved the treaty but without a vote to spare and subject to the removal of Article XII. The President delayed ratification, finding serious objections to the document that Jay had signed. During the anxious months of indecision he weighed two notably thoughtful papers prepared by Alexander Hamilton and Edmund Randolph. Both recommended favorable action, but Randolph made his approval subject to the British withdrawal of a recently issued order for the seizure of all corn, grain and flour destined for France. Washington agreed to the condition laid down by his Secretary of State.

. . . . .

Historians have sometimes said that the troubled situation in Europe would have restrained the British from provoking war. The Hamiltonians did not fear that the British would deliberately make war, but they did fear that the American government would be pushed into more and more extreme measures until the British would feel that they had no alternative. The Jay Treaty outlawed some of the extreme measures contemplated by the agrarians and also deprived the agrarians of much of their ammunition. The Northwest posts would no longer serve to stimulate anti-British feelings and compensation for losses on the high seas would take the sting out of British seizures. The Hamiltonians believed that the treaty would prevent war because it made the British connection more nearly palatable.

After the President ratified the treaty, the opposition determined to carry on the fight in the House of Representatives. A resolution introduced early in March 1796 called on the President to submit to the House the papers relating to the treaty. Immediately a debate, destined to last more than a month, ensued. Supporters of the treaty maintained that the lower branch had no power to act on treaties. The opponents sought to prove the contrary by two lines of argument. First, they contended that if they lacked the power, it meant that the Executive and the Senate acting in cooperation with a foreign power could make laws for the United States by means of treaties. Secondly, they argued that since Congress had the power to regulate commerce, any treaty containing commercial provisions must be subject to the approval of both branches of the legislature. James Madison granted that the Constitution gave the President the power, with the advice and consent of the Senate, to make treaties. This did not deprive the House, he said, of the power to consider the treaty when voting provisions for carrying it into effect. On March 24 the House voted 62 to 37 in favor of the resolution calling on the President to lay the papers of the negotiation before the House. Five days later the President notified the House that he could not do so.

Thereupon the House voted 57 to 36 in favor of the resolution maintaining its power to pass on any treaty that required laws to put it into effect. A debate on the treaty itself than ensued. James Madison found objections to almost every article. Great Britain should have been made to pay for the losses incurred from her continued occupation of the military posts. The treaty yielded the American claim for compensation due for the slaves taken away. The treaty provisions permitting free entry of goods for the Indians from Canada guaranteed British control of the fur trade and an influence over the Indians. The treaty ignominiously surrendered the principle of "free ships make free goods." The article prohibiting sequestration of debts deprived the United States of a defensive weapon. The right to add to the tonnage duties on British ships had been given up and thereby the power to stimulate the growth of an American merchant marine surrendered.

Hamilton had made the danger of war a chief argument for approval, but Madison found this danger "too visionary and incredible to be admitted into the question." Great Britain could find no just grounds for war in a decision to decline a treaty because it failed to provide for American interests. And why would Great Britain, beset by powerful enemies, add to the list the best customer for her manufactured products? To believe England capable of such action was, thought Madison, to accuse her of madness.

The anti-treaty leaders ridiculed the idea of war. Much of their argument rested on the troubled situation in Europe, but they also counted heavily on the strength of the United States as a deterrent to the British. The British West Indies were dependent on supplies from the United States. The British would also have to reckon with the fact that the United States was England's best customer. Wilson C. Nicholas of Virginia said "it is not to be believed that she would embark in a new war, with the sacrifice of her best trade; more especially, as she has shown an intention of making her remaining efforts against France, in the neighborhood of the United States, where their supplies will be essentially necessary to her success." William Giles found Great Britain too embarrassed by her situation in Europe to contemplate war against the United States. Americans, said Giles, would not "tremble at the sound of war from a nation thus circumstanced." He thought that Great Britain also placed greater value on trade with the United States than some would admit.

The argument against the treaty rode high on nationalistic passions. The agrarians paid scant attention to British arguments on the issues involved. They viewed each point from the vantage of America and rejected every compromise. Only a British surrender on almost all points could have satisfied the agrarians. Their ethno-centric view made it easy to find nothing but evils in the treaty. Yet, their antagonism did not rise out of purely nationalistic considerations.

The Jay Treaty pinched the Jeffersonians at three points. It committed the United States not to establish discriminatory duties against the British. Thereby it forced the agrarians to lay aside their whole foreign policy program and to accept that of the opposition.

Secondly, the treaty offended the nationalistic and democratic sentiments of the agrarians. Jefferson lamented: "The rights, the interest, the honor and faith of our nation are so grossly sacrificed. . . ." He wrote to Madison: "Where a faction has entered into a conspiracy with the enemies of their country to chain down the legislature at the feet of both; where the whole mass of our constituents have condemned this work in unequivocal manner, and are looking to you as their last hope to save them from the effects of the avarice and corruption of the first agent. . . ." Both Jefferson and Madison believed that a majority of the people opposed the treaty and that the popular will had been denied. When it became clear that the House of Representatives would appropriate the funds for putting the treaty into effect, Madison attributed it to the pressure of business interests.

Jefferson's and Madison's denunciations of the treaty are also better understood if one takes into account that in their eyes the treaty surrendered a major principle in the "Law of Nations." That term—"Law of Nations"—had all the aura of the Age of Enlightenment. It had no well defined meaning and certainly few generally accepted points, but to Jefferson and Madison it connoted justice and reason. They never doubted that their own broad interpretation of neutral rights accorded with the "Law of Nations" and the welfare of mankind.

This approach, one of the central threads of their foreign policy from 1789 to 1812, owed something to the fact that American interests would have benefitted tremendously by a universal acceptance of their interpretation of neutral rights. It owed quite as much to an idealistic view of what would benefit mankind. They desperately wanted a world order in which the innocent by-stander nations would not be made to suffer because a few major powers engaged in the folly of war. Jefferson and Madison overlooked the fact that Great Britain could not accept such an ideal without granting victory to its enemies.

In the situation confronting the United States in the spring of 1796 the surrender of the ideal had an additional and more grievous meaning for Jefferson's followers. To yield to British dictates on control of the seas meant that France would be denied access to American supplies. The United States would provide Great Britian with supplies at a time when the traditional friend, France, was struggling for liberty.

In September, 1796, George Washington delivered his Farewell Address. The President, finding himself amid the dissensions of heated party strife, had striven manfully to avoid falling into the hands of either faction. In 1793 he had, to a great degree, followed Jefferson's advice in meeting the dangers brought on by the war between Great Britain and France. Throughout the heated debates he had retained a sense of gratitude toward France and a sincere desire to deal with her justly. In the summer of 1795, he had resisted the pressure of Hamilton to ratify the Jay Treaty at once and had deliberated long before making his decision to ratify it. To be sure he could not participate in the feelings experienced by Jefferson and Madison because he did not share their philosophical outlook and their intense concern for their particular political ideals. On the other hand, he found it more difficult than Hamilton to make the concessions necessary to preserve harmony with Great Britain. The President found himself in an isolated position.

When the time came to deliver a farewell address, he called on Hamilton to draft it, and the message warned against party spirit and against a passionate attachment to one nation. To the more extreme elements in the more extreme Republican societies the counsel was applicable, but it scarcely applied to Jefferson and

Madison whose pro-French feelings were rigorously subordinated to American nationalism.

Their nationalism posed a danger for they confused their American view of the world with their proclaimed universal view of justice and right reason. Their strong desire to make their republic an example of what could be achieved by noble aspiration set free to apply reason made them impatient and particularly so concerning Great Britain's financial influence and arbitrary dicta as to how far the seas were to be open to a free exchange of goods. That they were misunderstood, that their views were dubbed theoretical, is not surprising. Idealists in the realm of foreign affairs trying to establish a program that would reconcile national interests and idealistic considerations were to find themselves in a difficult position many times in the future.

In the heated controversy over the Jay Treaty a set of symbols emerged that transferred the argument from the realm of the rational to the irrational. Followers of Hamilton were quickly denounced as monocrats; followers of Jefferson and Madison were identified as the dangerous disciples of the French school of reason. In the pamphlet warfare parties became images of the British or French systems. It was not only that Jefferson and Madison differed from Hamilton in the measures to be pursued but that the opponents read into them steps in the direction of a society patterned after popular conceptions of France and England. The differences between the foreign policies of the Federalists and Republicans had little relationship to the stereotypes of partisan political rhetoric. These widened the gulf beyond that warranted by a rather undramatic difference over practical measures.

A difference in basic attitudes also contributed to the political warfare. Thomas Jefferson and James Madison had no fear of society falling victim to instability, of individuals and factions irresponsibly following the whim of the moment, or of the social fabric being torn apart by the passions of men. Their confidence in the good sense of the body politic made a significant difference. When they encountered human foibles or systems that appeared to favor one group in society or one nation they boldly presumed that it was their duty to enlighten the misled and to change the system.

The Federalists certainly benefitted more directly from the measures of Hamilton and the close association with Great Britain, but that alone does not explain their stand on the Jay Treaty. They saw the social fabric as a frail gauze in constant danger of being torn apart. The British structure was their model because it gave stability to society and an orderly financial system that emphasized contracts, law and order. They saw no reason to risk present advantages for an untried experiment in reordering the nation's economic relations with the outside world, especially when to do so would align the nation with France. Hamilton's arguments in favor of the Jay Treaty rested on an acceptance of the world as it was and not on a vague concept of the world as it ought to be. Madison judged the Jay Treaty in terms of American rights and interests without making any concessions to the hard and fast economic realities. Hamilton succeeded in putting the problem of relations with Great Britain on the shelf. His whole argument centered on prudence; Madison's argument centered on what he believed to be just American claims.

3   FROM   *Felix Gilbert*
To the Farewell Address:
Ideas of Early American Foreign Policy

When Washington retired from office he left a nation still beset by domestic problems and faced with foreign dangers. He was determined to bequeath to the nation not only the legacy of his contribution to its creation, but also the wisdom of his judgment on the future course which it might pursue. Therefore he composed a farewell address to the nation. A large part of it was concerned with domestic rather than foreign affairs. The President had seen the dangers that excessive partisanship and violent domestic division could inflict. He warned his countrymen against intolerance and spite and cautioned them against the excesses of political parties.

His advice on foreign affairs was equally candid and forthright. And it is for this that his address is chiefly remembered. He warned against entering into permanent alliances, but urged that those properly agreed to be honored. He did not call for absolute neutrality and did not suggest that the United States never enter into a treaty with a European nation. He did argue against permanent alliances and did call for equal and impartial treatment toward all countries.

The reasons for the address and the role that Hamilton played in its drafting are carefully described and analyzed by Professor Felix Gilbert in his To The Farewell Address.

SOURCE. Felix Gilbert, *To the Farewell Address: Ideas of Early American Foreign Policy*, pp. 120–136. Copyright © 1961 by Princeton University Press. Reprinted by permission of Princeton University Press and the author.

WASHINGTON'S FAREWELL ADDRESS, 1796

Although the debate in the House over the Jay Treaty in March and April 1786 had shown the strength of partisan divisions in the field of foreign policy, the result was not entirely negative. Positively, the outcome of the debate represented an approval of the foreign policy of the government, and it had also clarified the constitutional issues involved in the conduct of foreign policy. Washington could rightly consider that if his first administration had established the foundations for the internal organization of the republic, his second administration had laid out the course for the management of foreign affairs. In May, Washington was free to turn again to the problems of his valedictory address. He sent his draft of a valedictory address to Alexander Hamilton, on whom he was accustomed to rely for help in the composition of state documents. This draft represented no great change from the ideas which he had expressed in February. In the first part of the draft, Washington reproduced the valedictory address which Madison had prepared for him in 1792. Then there followed a new part which, as Washington wrote to Hamilton, had become necessary because of "considerable changes having taken place both at home and abroad." The addition shows that Washington regarded the events in the field of foreign affairs as the central issues of his second administration.

II

The tone of the part which Washington had written to complement Madison's draft was very different from that of the valedictory of 1792. Taking a stand high above concrete and disputed political issues and expressing generally acceptable sentiments, Madison had woven together a justification of Washington's decision to retire, a praise of the American Constitution, and an exhortation to preserve the advantages of the Union.

In the part which Washington added in 1796, the closeness and the bitterness of the political fights of the preceding months and years were clearly noticeable. The last five paragraphs of this section mentioned the attacks against the government and the abuses to which the President had been subjected. Washington's statement that his "fortune, in a pecuniary point of view, has received no augmentation from my country" showed how he had been hurt by the recent criticisms resulting from revelations according to which he had temporarily overdrawn his accounts with the government. The section which stands between Madison's draft and the last five paragraphs of personal defense, and which forms the most important part of Washington's addition, is the section in which foreign policy has the most prominent role.

It consists of a number of different, only loosely connected thoughts, moulded in the form of a list of "wishes," as Washington himself called them. Of these nine wishes, only the first two and the last are not directly concerned with foreign policy. However, the first wish—an admonition to extinguish or, at least, moderate party disputes—and the last—a counsel to maintain the constitutional delimitations of powers—were inspired by developments in the area of foreign policy, by the bitterness of party differences revealed in the debate over the Jay Treaty, and by the attempt of the House to have a part in the making of treaties. The remaining six wishes, which refer to issues of foreign policy, summarized Washington's experiences in his second administration. Essentially, they were ideas which Washington had expressed at other places in the same or similar form. Washington's first three recommendations in the field of foreign affairs—scrupulously to observe treaty obligations, to refrain from political connections, and to take pride in America as a distinct nation—can be found, more briefly but in the same sequence, in a letter from Washington to Patrick Henry in October 1795. In his draft for the valedictory, Washington elaborated on the dangers of foreign interference in American politics and on the necessity of realizing that in foreign affairs, each nation is guided exclusively by egoistic motives. The following wish—that America must do everything possible to keep the peace for twenty years, until which time her position would be almost unassailable—was a revision of a paragraph in a letter from Washington to Gouverneur Morris of December 22, 1795. The last two pieces of advice—the need for maintaining a truly neutral attitude and for preserving the Union as a check against destructive intentions of foreign powers—Washington had also voiced previously.

The part of Washington's draft dealing with foreign affairs represents a collection of diverse thoughts and ideas which are neither closely integrated nor systematically organized. Yet one theme permeates the various paragraphs: a warning against the spirit of faction and against the danger of letting ideological predilections and prejudices enter considerations of foreign policy. This is the topic of the central paragraph in Washington's list of "wishes," where he admonished the citizens to take "pride in the name of an American." The same theme appears in the paragraphs on the duties of neutrals and the need for union; it is impressively stated as Washington's first "wish," in which he implored the citizens to use "charity and benevolence" towards each other in case of political differences and dissensions.

Washington did not provide an analysis of the international situation into which America had been placed. Nor did he describe the course which, as a result of such an analysis, America ought to follow in foreign policy. He touched upon these points, but only lightly and selectively, almost accidentally. Washington's fundamental concern was the attitude of American citizens towards foreign policy and the need for overcoming party spirit in decisions on foreign policy.

III

Washington's condemnation of the spirit of faction arose from a deep political conviction. Although differences in political opinions might be unavoidable, Washington believed that rational discussion would always lead to a realization of the true interest of the nation. Washington saw himself standing above the parties, forcing the contentious politicians to work together under the uniting banner of the true national interest. He had tried to keep Jefferson and Hamilton in the government even when their political differences had nearly paralyzed the functioning of the administration.

In 1796, it was an equally strange idea to bring Hamilton and Madison together in a common task. One cannot help wondering whether, in giving both Hamilton and Madison a part in the composition of his valedictory, Washington might have hoped that he could make this document a further demonstration of his conviction that party contrasts did not exclude cooperation in a situation of national interest and that this cooperation would lend added weight to his valedictory pronouncement, securing it against the objection of being an expression of personal or partisan views.

During the preceding years, Hamilton and Madison had emerged as the leaders of the two opposing parties, the Federalists and the Republicans. Both parties maintained that their differences were irreconcilable, because each believed the other was trying to overthrow the Constitution. To the Republicans, Washington had become an enemy, a prisoner of the Federalists. On the other hand, the Federalists, who characterized Madison as an irresponsible radical, could not look approvingly upon the possible increase in Madison's reputation resulting from his collaboration in Washington's valedictory.

When, in February 1796, Washington had told Hamilton of his plan of issuing a valedictory which would consist of two parts, the one which Madison had drafted in 1792 and the other an addition for which he asked Hamilton's assistance, Hamilton expressed his reservations immediately. Hamilton preferred an entirely new document; he seems also to have raised special objections to the contents of Madison's draft and to the mention of Madison's name in the valedictory.

But Washington stuck to his plan. On May 12, 1796, Washington invited Madison to dinner, probably to talk with him about his retirement. Washington might have thought he could hardly use Madison's draft for a valedictory, still less in a changed form, without informing him. Although Madison might have felt little enthusiasm for collaborating with Washington at a time when he was sharply opposed to the President's policy, he certainly had no valid reason for objecting. The valedictory of 1792 had been written in close adherence to Washington's instructions and placed at Washington's disposal.

Three days later, on May 15, 1796, Washington sent to Hamilton material for revision which consisted of a brief introduction, Madison's draft, and the lengthy addition necessitated by the "considerable changes having taken place both at home and abroad." Washington had made a concession to Hamilton's views by omitting, contrary to his original intention, a direct mention of Madison's name and by leaving out a few passages from Madison's draft. Moreover, the President permitted Hamilton "to throw the whole into a different form." But as Washington indicated, he preferred his original idea of a valedictory address which contained the draft of 1792 and his recently composed additions. Even if Hamilton should decide to give the valedictory an entirely new form, he should submit at the same time another draft which would be restricted to emendations and corrections of the papers Washington had sent him.

After the debate on the Jay Treaty in the House, which had increased party bitterness, Hamilton must have found the idea of Madison's associating with Washington in the announcement of the President's retirement more inappropriate than ever. Moreover, the high praise of Republican government contained in Maidson's draft could be interpreted as favoring an attitude to which Hamilton was violently opposed, that of placing America on the side of the French Revolution.

Thus Hamilton was anxious to dissuade Washington from letting the valedictory appear in the form Washington intended. Hamilton could hardly leave this to chance; thus he deliberately employed a method which promised a politically successful outcome. Instead of starting his work by amending and correcting the material which Washington had sent him, he first wrote an entirely new draft, making free use of Washington's permission to "throw the whole into a different form." On July 30, Hamilton was able to send this new draft to Washington with an accompanying letter in which he said that he was now beginning with his work on the second part of Washington's request, namely, with the corrections and improvements of the papers which Washington had sent him in May. However, he added immediately that "I confess the more I have considered the matter the less eligible this plan has appeared to me. There seems to be a certain awkwardness in the thing. . . . Besides that, I think that there are some ideas which will not wear well in the former address.. . ." The presentation of an entirely new and carefully worked out draft, combined with deprecatory remarks about Washington's original plan, did its work. When, on August 10, Hamilton sent to Washington a "draft for incorporating," as Hamilton called his revision of the material which Washington had sent him in May, Washington had become accustomed to the idea of using Hamilton's "Original Major Draft" for his valedictory address.

IV

Hamilton was at work on the "Original Major Draft" for Washington's valedictory from the second part of May till far into July. Hamilton's wife, in her old age, still remembered that "the address was written, principally at such times as his Office was seldom frequented by his clients and visitors, and during the absence of his students to avoid interruption; at which times he was in the habit of calling me to sit with him, that he might read to me as he wrote, in order, as he said, to discover how it sounded upon the ear, and making the remark, 'My dear Eliza, you must be to me what Molière's old nurse was to him.' " The care and deliberateness with which Hamilton proceeded suggests that he was impressed by the importance as well as by the difficulty of the task.

Among the considerations which influenced Hamilton in the composition of the document, his eagerness to avoid inserting Madison's valedictory of 1792 was only one, and probably not the most important one. Despite the attacks against Washington in the last years of his second term, the President enjoyed still greater authority and reputation than any other American political leader; the thoughts which he would express when he announced his final retirement from office were bound to make a deep impact on American political thinking. Hamilton must have been well aware that participation in the drafting of Washington's valedictory gave him a unique opportunity to impress on the minds of Americans some of his favorite political ideas. But he was certainly not guided exclusively by personal ambition and party interest. For almost twenty years, Hamilton had been Washington's close collaborator, and he must have felt a selfless obligation to give a dignified form to the final political manifesto of the man whom he had served and admired. Yet Hamilton's work was made still more difficult because he knew that although Washington had little confidence in his own literary gifts, he was a man of "strong penetration" and "sound judgment." Washington would not place his name under a document which he could not regard as an expression of his own mind and ideas.

Thus Hamilton's draft, although very different from the material which Washington had sent him, embodied in form and substance much of Washington's draft. A paper has been preserved which permits an insight into Hamilton's working methods: an "abstract of points to form an address." It lists 23 points containing brief statements of the issues with which he wanted to deal, presenting them more or less in the sequence of the Farewell Address. Of these 23 points, 13 are brief excerpts or paraphrases of Washington's draft. In the middle, from the 10th to the 19th point, Hamilton abandoned close adherence to Washington's draft, enlarging Washington's ideas and adducing new material. Thus the list of points reveals that although Hamilton did not accept Washington's plan of inserting Madison's draft of 1792 as a whole, he had few objections to the ideas outlined by Madison and Washington; indeed, he was willing to incorporate them almost literally. However, he felt the document should be strengthened; it ought to receive more body and substance.

This view is confirmed by the form which Hamilton's draft finally took. The first eight paragraphs, announcing Washington's intention to retire from political life and expressing his wishes for the future prosperity of America under a free constitution, are closely modeled 'after Washington's draft. Then Hamilton let Washington say, "Here perhaps I ought to stop." But he did not do so, because solicitude for the welfare of the American people urged him "to offer some sentiments the result of mature reflection confirmed by observation and experience which appear to me essential to the permanency of your felicity as a people"; these sentiments should be received as "the disinterested advice of a parting friend."

With these sentences Hamilton launched a discussion leading far beyond the thoughts contained in Washington's draft. From the point of view of contents as well as from the point of view of length, this section gave the Farewell Address its real weight.

After this, Hamilton returned to a phraseology startlingly similar to that which he had used in introducing the section; he said that "in offering to you, my countrymen, these counsels of an old and affectionate friend—counsels suggested by laborious reflection, and matured by a various experience, I dare not hope that they will make the strong and lasting impressions I wish. . . ." Then there followed six paragraphs of personal justification, which in contents and phraseology were patterned after the end of Washington's draft.

Thus Hamilton's chief contribution to Washington's Farewell Address was the central section of the document, which replaced the "list of wishes" of Washington's draft. Nevertheless, the theme of Washington's list of wishes, the warning against partisanship in foreign policy, was fully expressed; however, it was set in the wider framework of a general survey of domestic and foreign policy.

Hamilton gave the greatest attention to the section on foreign policy. Whereas the reflections on domestic policy corresponded to the outline given in his "abstract of points," the statement on foreign policy was entirely remodeled.

The transition from domestic policy to foreign policy followed smoothly from a warning against party spirit which opens the door to intrigues by foreigners and may lead to attachments in which the smaller nation will revolve around the larger one "as its satellite."

At this point, Hamilton repeated Washington's advice to "avoid connecting ourselves with the politics of any Nation." Hamilton was somewhat more cautious than Washington. He recommended having "as little political connection . . . as possible." Departing from

Washington's draft, Hamilton did not say anything at this point about commercial relations but rather went on to justify the advice to abstain from political connections.

The necessity for this attitude, Hamilton believed, followed from the natural situation of things. Each state has certain fundamental interests which it must follow in its policy. If states are in close proximity to each other, their interests touch upon each other and clashes are unavoidable. If America were to ally herself with one of the European powers, she would inevitably have to participate in every European conflict. Such a connection with European power politics would be "artificial"; America was so distant from Europe that she did not belong "naturally" to the European system. From this analysis, Hamilton deduced a "general principle of policy" for America. Although in particular emergencies America might be forced to make a temporary alliance, permanent alliances must be avoided. In its practical consequences, this was not very different from what Washington had said in his draft. But Washington had stressed the weakness of the United States which, within the next twenty years, would make involvement in a war extremely dangerous for the existence of the young republic. By removing the time limit from this piece of advice, by basing it on unchangeable geographical conditions, and by presenting it as a principle of policy, Hamilton made the recommendation in his draft weightier, more impressive, and more apodictic.

It is significant that Hamilton treated with commerce after he had discussed the question of alliances. To him, regulation of commercial relations remained subordinated to power politics. Although America's aim should be the widest possible liberalization of commerce, a certain flexibility in practice was necessary. Commerce was a weapon in the struggle of power politics; in the arrangement of their commercial relations, nations did not follow idealistic principles but only their interests. With the exhortation to recognize national egoism as the driving force in international relations, Hamilton concluded the "counsels of an old and affectionate friend."

In its terminology and formulations, the section on foreign policy echoed expressions and thoughts which had dominated the discussion of foreign affairs ever since America had entered the scene of foreign policy in 1776. We are reminded of Paine's *Common Sense*. We find the word *"entangle"* which in America had developed into a technical term for characterizing the dangerous consequences of involvement in European politics. We see the distinction between "artificial" and "natural" connections, reflecting the Enlightenment belief in a progress from a world of power politics to an era of permanent peace and increasing prosperity. We recall the famous resolution of Congress of 1783 that "the true interest of these states requires that they should be as little as possible entangled in the politics and controversies of European nations."

This use, in the Farewell Address, of terms and concepts which had been continuously applied in the discussion of foreign affairs might have been intentional. Hamilton might have felt that these reflections would be more acceptable if they appeared as a restatement of currently held views rather than as a presentation of new ideas. But behind this façade of customary terms and concepts, there was a structure of thought which was Hamilton's own.

Whether Hamilton drafted this part of the Farewell Address with the help of documents which he had previously written, or whether the similarities to his previous works on foreign policy came from such firm and definite convictions that they always took the same expression, we cannot know. In any case, just a year before Hamilton began to work on the Farewell Address, he wrote under the name Horatius a defense of the Jay Treaty which contained a warning against entanglement "in all the contests, broils and wars of Europe" in words very similar to those used in the Farewell Address. Some of the formulations which the Farewell Address and the Horatius paper have in common can also be found in the Memorandum of September 15, 1790, the first written presentation of Hamilton's opinions on foreign affairs as a member of Washington's Cabinet. In this search for ancestors of the Farewell Address among Hamilton's previous writings, we might go back still further to the *Federalist*.

There are passages in Hamilton's draft of the Farewell Address which correspond closely to ideas in the *Federalist*, making it almost certain that Hamilton had this book not only on his bookshelf— as would have been a matter of course—but also on his writing desk when he drafted the Farewell Address. The warning in the Address against wars resulting from the passions of people was a restatement of Hamilton's argument in the sixth number of the *Federalist*, that "there have been . . . almost as many popular as royal wars." Stylistic similarities also exist between the eleventh number of the *Federalist* and passages of the Farewell Address on foreign policy. Ideas which in the Address were only vaguely adumbrated were more clearly expressed in the eleventh number of the *Federalist*. In the Farewell Address, emphasis was laid on Europe's possessing a special political system; the consequence of this point—that America had a political system of her own—was only suggested. The statement in the eleventh number of the *Federalist* that the United States ought "to aim at an ascendant in the system of American affairs" revealed Hamilton's full thought. Because Washington hardly would have liked this open announcement of an aggressive imperialist program, Hamilton refrained from expressing this idea explicitly in the Farewell Address.

The relationship between the Farewell Address and the *Federalist* is particularly important because it shows that although Hamilton used Washington's ideas and statements of others, he placed them in a different setting and gave them a new meaning.

The law of action propounded by Hamilton in the Farewell Address was presented as the specific application of general laws ruling in the political world. It was derived from the geographical division of the earth and from the principle which dominated the life of every state: striving to increase power in line with its fundamental interests. States situated in the same geographical area were tied together in a continous power struggle arising from clashing interests. They were members of the same political system which extended as far as its natural geographical limits. In Hamilton's formulation, the warning against connection with European power politics was derived neither from a fear of strengthening the centrifugal forces in American political life, as it dominated Washington's thoughts, nor from utopian hopes in an imminent end of the era of power politics and national division, as the founders of American independence had hoped. To Hamilton, sovereign states, competition among them, and power politics were necessary factors in social life; successful political action depended on proceeding according to these presuppositions. Hamilton presented his advice as the necessary consequence of political science; he conceived it as an application of the eternal laws of politics to the American situation. The separation of America from Europe's foreign policy was desirable not because it might be the beginning of a change, of a reform of diplomacy, but because it corresponded to what the political writers had discovered about the political practice of the time. The intellectual framework of the recommendations on foreign policy in the Farewell Address was that of the school of the interests of the state. This is reflected not only in the phraseology and the argumentation, but also in Hamilton's attempt to summarize these counsels in a "great rule of conduct," a "general principle."

When Hamilton sent his draft to Washington, he wrote that he had tried "to render this act importantly and lastingly useful." We can now better understand what these words meant. Hamilton wanted Washington to leave to his successors an explanation of the principles which had guided his policy, just as other rulers and statesmen of the eighteenth century were accustomed to doing in their Political Testaments. In revising Washington's draft for a valedictory, Hamilton transformed it into a Political Testament.

V

The "great rule" which Washington had set down in the Farewell Address served as a guide to American foreign policy for over a century; of all the Political Testaments of the eighteenth century, the Farewell Address alone succeeded in achieving practical political significance.

Some part of its influence is due to the "accidents of politics," to events in which the United States had, at best, a supporting role. The conflicts of the Napoleonic era and the weakening of the Spanish power broke the ring which foreign colonial possessions had laid around the territory of the United States. As long as several European states were close neighbors, the advice to avoid alliances was an ideal to be pursued rather than a feasible proposition. It became a workable policy only when effective rule by a foreign power was restricted to the north of the continent. The political separation of America from the European power struggle was strengthened by changes which took place in Europe. Nationalism and industrialism shifted the interests of the European powers, and the competition among them, into new channels. Thus, in the nineteenth century, conditions came into existence under which America's foreign policy could become a policy of isolation.

Nevertheless, the profound impact of Washington's counsels in the Farewell Address was also created by features inherent in the document itself. It was the first statement, comprehensive and authoritative at the same time, of the principles of American foreign policy. Hamilton based the discussion of foreign affairs in the Farewell Address on a realistic evaluation of America's situation and interests. Because Hamilton was opposed to American involvement in a war, to which the emotional attachment with France might lead, he emphasized the necessity of neutrality and peace. The Farewell Address, therefore, could repeat and absorb those views and concepts which expressed the mood of a more idealistic approach to foreign policy. These elements were not like ghost cities left abandoned outside the main stream of development; they were necessary stations on the road "to the Farewell Address."

Political Testaments, in general, remained closely tied to the eighteenth-century concept of power politics. The integration of idealistic assumptions constitutes the distinguishing feature of the Farewell Address. Thus it could have an appeal in the following century of rising democracy when foreign policy demanded legitimation by clearly felt and recognized values and needed to be conducted in accordance with the will of the people.

Because the Farewell Address comprises various aspects of American political thinking, it reaches beyond any period limited in time and reveals the basic issue of the American attitude toward foreign policy: the tension Idealism and Realism. Settled by men who looked for gain and by men who sought freedom, born into independence in a century of enlightened thinking and of power politics, America has wavered in her foreign policy between Idealism and Realism, and her great historical moments have occurred when both were combined. Thus the history of the Farewell Address forms only part of a wider, endless, urgent problem. This study is an attempt to shed light on its beginnings. With the analysis of the diverse intellectual trends which went into the making of the Farewell Address, with the description of its genesis, our story ends.

4 FROM   *Alexander DeConde*
The Quasi-War

The dangers of domestic strife and foreign involvement to which Washington had addressed himself were very nearly realized by his successor John Adams. It was, of course, only too easy to fall into the condition about which the retired President had warned. The tempo of the war in Europe had quickened by 1796, and the United States found herself increasingly damaged by the actions of both Britain and France. The familiar problems of impressment and the British Orders in Council had not disappeared, but the flagrant behavior of France was disturbingly new and unexpected. Indeed, the French seizure of American ships and their cargo reached such a degree that there were many in the United States who favored a war with her. There had always been Federalists whose sympathies with Britain ran so deep that they would have welcomed public support for her. But now, many of those who had supported the French Revolution, and had hoped for a victory by France in her war, turned against her. There were militant calls to arms, and it even appeared that President Adams was prepared to lead the charge. Certainly the affronts to America were many and the injuries she suffered great, but a war with France at this time would have ill suited American interests. President Adams soon realized this and began to dampen the feelings that he had once aroused.

Professor Alexander DeConde in his The Quasi-War *examines the conditions which led to this near rupture in Franco-American relations and analyzes the role played in it by John Adams.*

THE QUASI-WAR WITH FRANCE, 1797–1800

> *It must always happen, so long as America is an independent Republic or nation, that the balance of power will continue to be of the utmost importance to her welfare.*
>
> THOMAS ROYLSTON ADAMS, *October 1799*

A conclusion to an historical study, by summing up significant points, by cutting through detail here and there, and by stressing or reiterating interpretations, may aid the reader in looking back and gaining perspective on the work as a whole, as does the man who

SOURCE. Alexander DeConde, *The Quasi-War*, pp. 327–340. Copyright © 1966 Alexander DeConde. Reprinted with the permission of Charles Scribner's Sons and author.

climbs a mountain, gazes back, and realizes there is a unity in sky, mountain, river, and valley. Such historical perspective may in turn suggests that what the reader has just experienced, like the man on the mountain, while unique in time and particulars, is connected to a larger pattern. This conclusion, therefore, in addition to summing up, seeks to remind the reader that the history he has just read is not a fragment drifting alone in a world inhabited by academicians, but is part of a large, almost universal theme in the experience of civilized man, that of conflict, and especially of war and peace.

In this conflict with France we have had the example of a nation, the United States, perched on the brink of full-scale war, of stumbling toward, but not falling into, the inferno. The decisions that drove America and France—at the time the two most democratic large nations in the world—toward unqualified war were not thoughtfully planned, were not founded on all the available evidence, and were not the result of the careful weighing of various alternatives. Those decisions often flowed from the heated emotions, the irrational attitudes, and the disorderly thinking of excited and opinionated men.

Full-scale war, as we have seen, could not have brought profit to either nation. When emotions cooled, many statesmen on both sides of the Atalantic saw this. Peace ultimately prevailed for selfish, rational reasons. Men could gain more from it than from war. During the Quasi-War there was time, as there has not always been in acute international crises, for the rational to gain ascendancy over the irrational.

Unless a conqueror ruthlessly imposed peace, the diplomacy of peacemaking has always been complicated and time consuming. So it was during the long, and even tedious, Quasi-War, or what John Adams himself called "the half war with France."

One reason why the complicated peacemaking in this conflict has not previously attracted careful attention from scholars is that the Quasi-War was not a true war. Although both France and the United States were hurt by their hostilities, neither had proclaimed the other country a national enemy. Even at the height of the crisis France treated the United States more as a hostile neutral than as an enemy state.

In many ways this conflict proved more frustrating than a war fought by massed battalions and organized naval squadrons. It placed the Adams administration and the American people in a state of almost perpetual crisis. They found themselves caught in a wave of political agitation and hysterical patriotism that brought neither the emotional outlet of war nor the satisfactions of peace. The very nature of this struggle with France, like the head of Janus facing two ways, contributed to the turbulence of Adams's Presidency.

Extremists in the President's own party embraced the conflict with France, tried to expand it, and wanted to use it politically as a partisan, one-party crusade. They considered France a land of wild-eyed Jacobins, and looked upon those Americans who opposed their program as domestic Jacobins or, at best, dupes of foreign Jacobins. The irrational antipathy of these Federalist extremists to France led them to believe that the war they favored would serve, not injure, the national interest.

Occupying positions of leadership in the Federalist party and in the government, these men wanted an unqualified declaration of war against France. In their view, and in that of later writers who approved of their actions, if ever "there existed a righteous and good ground for war since the institution of nations, it existed in the year 1798." The extreme Federalists tried to, and did, use their party's control of foreign policy as a weapon against Republicans. Anything that kept Jacobins out of office, even war, they seemed to think, was proper and patriotic.

These war hawks found it easy to assume the role of patriots seeking to avenge national honor. Justice appeared to be on their side. Other Americans could join them in their hatred of a foreign country and, of course, add to their own sense of "belonging" to a national cause. Such identification was satisfying, for one did not have to be an extremist or a war hawk to take pride in his young country's defiance of powerful France in 1798. These Federalist patriots of 1798 were among the new nation's first powerful, noisy, flag-waving, and intolerant nationalists.

The unyielding resistance of the United States to France not only swelled national pride, as a British observer commented, but it also raised America's status "in the estimation of foreign powers." All Europe, according to William Vans Murray, viewed America's resort to naval combat with astonishment and respect. Then, with a chauvinism befitting any dedicated nationalist, he claimed that the United States "appears in the Splendour of a great nation," its reputation exalted.

Republicans, while probably no less patriotic, or nationalistic, but at this time less chauvinistic, from the beginning opposed the Federalist program. Even as the crisis mounted and American seamen fought French sailors, Republicans denied that the country was at war, pointing out that only Congress had the right to declare war, and that it had never done so against France. High Federalists, on the other hand, claimed that the battles at sea had grown into actual war, and they tried to justify their measures against France, and even those against fellow Americans, such as the Alien and Sedition laws, on the basis of a wartime emergency.

Political feeling on the nature of the Quasi-War ran deep, so much so that in 1800 the Supreme Court, when faced with problems arising out of French spoliations of American commerce and retaliatory legislation passed by Congress, chose to define what kind of an enemy France was. In the case of *Bas v. Tingy* the court held that a state of "limited, partial war" existed, and that hence France was legally an enemy nation. Since this decision sustained the view of Federalists, they applauded.

Republicans, however, reacted with a withering hostility. They argued, apparently for the first time in the nation's history, that a judge could or should be impeached for rendering so partisan a decision. Philadelphia's *Aurora* stated, for instance, that in this case the decision was "most important and momentous to the country, and in our opinion every Judge who asserted we were in a state of war. contrary to the rights of Congress to declare it, *ought to be impeached.*'

Regardless of partisan debate and judicial opinion, it is clear that those who clamored for unlimited hostilities, and who were determined to keep the door bolted against peace, never gained full command of both the executive and legislative branches of government at one time. Not even at the height of the XYZ frenzy did diplomacy between France and the United States altogether stop, or hostilities completely take over. The reasons for this, and hence why full-scale war did not come, are woven into a web of international and domestic politics.

Why Peace Came

Some contemporaries, mainly Federalists and foreign observers such as the British, summarized the reasons why actual war did not break out in a simple concept of force met by counterforce. "The firmness and vigor of the United States, in all probability, has prevented a war with France," an anonymous British commentator explained. "The French calculated upon their party in America, and they were disappointed. This was the scourge of war which they threatened. Without this they are impotent. By entering into a war with America, they can do no more mischief than they have already done by their cruisers."

The French, on the other hand, believed that their forbearance and their military strength had prevented the United States from allying itself with Britain in a full-scale war. The "brilliant [military] situation of France," Léombe maintained, had kept Adams from being pushed into an unrestricted war against France, and against Spain too.

It is true that the French had changed their policy toward the United States when Talleyrand took office and had become very conciliatory after the X Y Z fiasco. According to their theory of wise forbearance and patience, their careful diplomacy had thwarted English plans to involve the United States in an enlarged war with France, had defeated the scheme of High Federalists to bait them into declaring war and hence stigmatize them as aggressors, and had succeeded in changing American policy so that Adams became willing to send the Ellsworth mission to Paris. Talleyrand, who gave French policy continuity despite upheavals within the government, stressed his country's forbearance in contrast to American belligerence. "I do not know why it is that at each step towards reconciliation," he wrote, "a cause of irritation intervenes and that these are always begun by the United States."

On the American side the question of war or peace had become a central issue in the party politics of an emerging modern democracy. That issue, therefore, became less susceptible to central control than in France, and in America the reasons why unrestricted war failed to erupt became more complex than in France. Three of the more important of these American reasons were public opposition to unrestrained hostilities, expressed politically through Republicans and through moderate Federalists in Congress, the changed attitude of President Adams himself, and the patient diplomacy of negotiators in Paris.

Adams's own policies had not led to the Quasi-War. He had inherited the crisis from President Washington and had tried immediately to resolve it through negotiation. When this effort failed Adams aligned himself with the extremists of his own party and went along with their war program. Yet Adams did not, as many party leaders wanted him to do, ask Congress for a declaration of war. He hesitated not because he believed in peace at all costs, but because a part of him recoiled at the thought of leading a disunited country into unlimited hostilities. Wishing to have behind him a popular sentiment strong enough to overcome Republican opposition to war, he wanted to be sure Congress would vote for a declaration of war before he asked for one. He realized that the internal opposition to an enlarged conflict was so widespread that revolution, with American pitted against American, might follow if public support could not be built up for a declaration of war.

Even Hamilton, whose attitude toward full-scale war, over a period of three years, swung like a pendulum, finally recognized that public opinion so strongly favored peace that the government could not ignore this sentiment. "Of one thing I am sure," he wrote when he learned that peace was probable, "If France will slide into a state of Peace *de facto*, we must meet her on that ground. The actual posture of European Affairs and the opinions of our people demand an accommodating course."

Even at the height of the X Y Z crisis, with public sentiment toward France heated and belligerently hostile, the people were divided in their attitude toward naked war. Later, Federalists realized that the masses would sympathize with Adams's peace moves. So moderate Federalists, at least, bowed to public opinion.

Ironically, many of the merchants and shipowners who bore the brunt of French spoliations were among those most opposed to war. Despite the French attacks on their property, while Britain and France fought and the United States remained technically neutral, these merchants prospered.

Like the merchants, American diplomats were willing to endure much for peace. First Marshall, Pinckney, and Gerry, and especially Gerry, then Ellsworth, Davie, and Murray, and finally Murray alone, stretched their powers rather than risk the loss of peace. Although Federalists, these diplomats were never as unbending or irrational toward the French as were the High Federalists, such as Pickering. This willingness of American negotiators to compromise and not seek refuge in the letter of instructions made possible the Convention of Môrtefontaine, and later its ratification by Napoleon Bonaparte. In these years American diplomats abroad were more willing to make decisions on their own when confronted with unexpected situations than would be negotiators in later years.

The success of the diplomats in obtaining peace upset the plans of High Federalists. These High Federalists had been disappointed, but not dismayed, when John Adams had not obtained a declaration of war from Congress. They, and the President himself at more than one point, had expected France to declare war, or at least, to commit acts so intolerable as to make full-scale hostilities inevitable. A war declared or forced by France, they reasoned, would unite the country in a crusade against Jacobinism, abroad and at home, and hence would be more desirable than one declared under presidential initiative. Although extreme Federalists waited impatiently, France never declared war or committed the final provocative act.

While Federalists waited for enlarged hostilities, animosities within their party became uncontrollable, and the drive toward war began to decelerate. These differences among party leaders, with Adams on one side and the Hamiltonians on the other, were not openly discernible when the President sent his first mission to France, but they were beneath the surface of party unity. Adams wanted the mission to succeed; the Hamiltonians expected it to fail. They wished to make use of that failure to discredit the Republican party and ultimately to obtain war. At more than one point Hamilton wanted to turn the defensive maritime struggle into a war of conquest. With some consistency, High Federalists tried to make war with France a key factor in their party's policy.

As President, Adams was crucial to this policy. Without his request for a declaration of war, High Federalists realized, they had practically no chance of carrying a majority in Congress for it. Congress has never declared war without a request from the President.

Not until after Adams broke with the Hamiltonians over the issue of rank in the Army did he become willing to listen to overtures for peace. Later, when he became fully aware of the extent of High Federalist opposition to him, he even became willing to risk strife within his party in an effort to obtain an honorable peace.

After recovering from the shock of the American reaction to the XYZ imbroglio, Talleyrand offered Adams a means of retreating gracefully from the brink of war. Talleyrand and other French statesmen did this and refused to take the final step into war, not because they loved the United States, but because full-blown hostilities could bring no advantage to France and possibly much harm. Within France, moreover, the idea of war against the United States had no popular support. In the French view unlimited war with the United States would have been a stinging nuisance, would have benefited only England, and would in no important way have served France's national interest.

When Talleyrand had control over foreign policy, therefore, he never allowed a complete rupture in diplomatic relations with the United States. He deliberately and carefully avoided giving the High Federalists a further pretext for war. His was a dangerous game, but it worked.

Talleyrand had not had a hand in the policy that had precipitated the Quasi-War. The French statesmen who had touched off the undeclared war had misjudged the extent of their country's influence in the United States, had underestimated the strength of the Federalist tie to England, and had misunderstood the emerging American national temper. As they had ever since the American Revolution, French statesmen had sought to use, to manipulate, or to take advantage of American politics to advance their own foreign policy. In 1797, to be specific, men such as Delacroix and Reubell had tried to destroy the Jay Treaty and to turn the United States against England. In 1798, when Talleyrand and others saw that this policy of threats and humiliation had merely united former friends of France in the United States with enemies, even to the point of war, the French government shifted its policy.

Persistence in this hostile course, the new men of the Directory had realized, would drive the United States into the arms of England. Later, after Napoleon Bonaparte became First Consul, took over the Directory's foreign policy, sought to build a maritime coalition against England, and planned to reconstruct an empire in North America, the friendship of the United States became important to French policy in a positive way.

France's effort to use the United States in the international policies of Europe and the American reaction to this policy, as well as to British policy, illustrates another historically significant point about the Federalist era. Leaders such as Adams realized that the politics of Europe's rulers, particularly of France and Britain, could vitally affect the United States. Adams, and those close to him, therefore, were not isolationist in their thinking. Isolationism, in the sense of the American government seeking to sever political, and even diplomatic, connections in Europe, became government policy after Jefferson took office.

. . . . .

The Convention of Môrtefontaine, however, was more important to the interests of the United States than to those of France. In the sense that the President had indicated that the Ellsworth mission would be his last effort at conciliation and if it failed there seemingly would be no alternative to actual war, it prevented full-scale war. That resolution of a frustrating conflict, despite the fact that the convention did not settle all the questions at issue with France to the satisfaction of many Americans, was in itself a major achievement.

In addition, the Convention of 1800 laid to rest the dispute over neutral rights with France that had risen out of the Jay Treaty. Before the Quasi-War France had been the most favored nation in America's treaty obligations, but now France accepted the loss of that status, and even accepted the Jay Treaty as a fact. This in itself constituted a considerable diplomatic accomplishment for the United States. The new convention removed the causes of irritation imbedded in the treaties of 1778 and the consular convention of 1788. It rescued all the ships and other property the French had taken but had not yet definitely condemned. More important, that treaty legally freed the United States from its first entangling alliance, an obligation that had seemingly grown more onerous with each passing year. Finally, the convention helped secure the goodwill of Bonaparte, and thus laid the groundwork for the acquisition of Louisiana two years later.

When Bonaparte sold Louisiana he stated, possibly with exaggerated emphasis, that he did so because, among other reasons, he wished to prevent misunderstandings with the United States. He and other French statesmen professed to regard the Louisiana Treaty, styled simply an act of amity between two friendly countries, as complementing the Convention of 1800. Regardless of the true depth of these sentiments, they do indicate that the convention was important in French policy, and that without it the United States might not have acquired Louisiana peacefully and cheaply, as it did in 1803.

For all this, the United States gave up claims against France which might never have been paid anyway. By almost any standard of measurement this peace settlement was a significant accomplishment for a young nation not yet able to place the independent weight on the scale of international power its own patriots, with exaggerated national pride, thought it could or should.

Under more difficult circumstances than in the negotiations in London in 1794 the Convention of Môrtefontaine secured more from France than England had conceded in the Jay Treaty, though John Jay did obtain compensation for shipping losses suffered at the hands of the British. No American, despite Adams's bellicosity, his desire several times to seek a declaration of war against France, his vacillating attitude toward peace overtures, his loose control over subordinates, and his feeling that his own people had repudiated him and his policies at the polls, contributed more to this diplomatic feat than did John Adams. As his son John Quincy pointed out, the elder Adams proved "that in your administration you were not the man of any party but of the whole nation."

John Adams recognized the importance of this contribution, for out of his many achievements near the close of his long life he chose, with strained simplicity, to stress this one. "I will defend my missions to France, as long as I have an eye to direct my hand, or a finger to hold my pen. They were the most disinterested and meritorious actions of my life. I reflect upon them with so much satisfaction, that I desire no other inscription over my gravestone than: 'Here lies John Adams, who took upon himself the responsibility of the peace with France in the year 1800.'"

Adams has often, and sometimes with exaggerated justification, been praised as the peacemaker, but another man whose contribution to peace in the period of the Quasi-War was greater, has seldom been thought of as the peacemaker. This is the sinuous Talleyrand, whose reputation for honesty is just the opposite of that of flinty John Adams. Perhaps this reputation for unscrupulousness has clouded everything Talleyrand touched. Yet in the crisis of the undeclared war Adams more often than he surrendered to emotions and strutted like a warrior. Both men, nonetheless, strove for peace over great obstacles before it was too late. Both were peacemakers.

As for the United States itself, peace with France, the escape from imperialistic ventures in the West Indies and Latin America, the dissolution of the alliance of 1778, and the ultimate acquisition of Louisiana, are among the most enduring diplomatic achievements of the republic. All flowed, in one way or another, from the Convention of Môrtefontaine. From the perspective of a century and three quarters it seems fair to conclude that perhaps no peace settlement has brought the nation greater benefits for so little cost.

5 FROM   *Lawrence Kaplan*

Jefferson and France

There are few single events in the history of the United States which so affected the future of that nation as the Louisiana Purchase. At one stroke America added a new dimension to her size, her prestige, and her sense of power. There were some who questioned the constitutionality and desirability of Jefferson's actions, but few who doubted its final wisdom. The necessity for swift action over Louisiana arose from Spain's transfer of that territory to France. On the day that France took possession of New Orleans, Jefferson wrote. "We must marry ourselves to the British fleet and nation." The reason for this was plain because if Napoleon recreated a French empire in the Mississippi, who would the United States have to turn to but England? But providence extended a hand to the United States, for Napoleon's army, which had been sent to Santo Domingo, was decimated by disease. This disaster checked France's ambition and, rather than see the recently acquired territory fall into the hands of Britain, she decided to dispose of it to the United States.

It was during this time that Jefferson sent Monroe to join Livingston in Paris with instructions to purchase New Orleans and as much of Florida east of the Mississippi as possible. To the astonishment of the Americans they were offered all of Louisiana and, after a period of haggling over the price, purchased this enormous and ill-defined area for only fifteen million dollars. News of this extraordinary coup was welcomed with jubilation in the west and with general satisfaction throughout the nation. Professor Lawrence Kaplan in his Jefferson and France *provides the most recent study of this most extraordinary event.*

THE LOUISIANA PURCHASE, 1803

Despite Pichon's errors of judgment, the Frenchman's fear of Jefferson's and of America's reaction to France's repossession of Louisiana was not inordinate. When the truth of France's intentions became known, the former Francophile picked up every weapon at his disposal, not excluding the threat of an alliance with Britain, to express his disapproval of France. Louisiana appeared to have been the final element in the evolution of Jefferson from party chieftain to national leader. If Bonaparte's rise to power had given

SOURCE. Lawrence Kaplan, *Jefferson and France* (New Haven: Yale University Press, 1967), pp. 96–104. Copyright © 1967 by Yale University. Reprinted by permission of the publisher and the author.

him doubts as to France's republicanism, the news about Louisiana had converted these doubts into fears, not for the future of French liberties but for the maintenance of American sovereignty.

Although France intended to conceal the fact of the Treaty of San Ildefonso until Louisiana had been fully secured, a secret involving such stakes was impossible to keep for long. Rumors of the transaction flew all over Europe, notably into the hands of the British enemy, who in turn relayed them to the Americans. Rufus King, the Federalist Minister to England, whom Jefferson was in no hurry to discharge, reported in March, 1801 the news that a double disaster awaited the United States: cession of Louisiana and the Floridas to France, and negotiation of a Franco-British peace which would enable Bonaparte to take advantage of his new property. When these tidings reached the United States, Jefferson confided to his friends the ominous implications that the transfer of Louisiana would have for American security.

From the moment he heard the news he began to wrestle with the problem of living next door to a new neighbor in control of New Orleans. It was an unhappy prospect he faced, filled with opportunities for violence in the event the French attempted to build an empire in America. Even if they did not intend to violate American territory, their probable interference with American commerce on the Mississippi would drive the Westerners either to war or to desertion of the Union. The solution for the United States lay only in Jefferson's ability to thwart fulfilment of the agreement between Spain and France. Such was his object.

War with France was one solution to the problem of Louisiana, but it was an unpalatable response for the President, considering his distaste for the cost of maintaining a large military establishment and considering his fear of a military caste which would thrive on war. The solution had to be a peaceable one, and in order to win time for working out a policy he appeared willing to accept the fiction that Louisiana was still Spanish. If he did not have to recognize the existence of a transfer, he would not have to take any immediate steps until France actually secured possession of the territory. In the meantime, it was conceivable that something could arise that would nullify the Franco-Spanish deal. Hence his annual message to Congress in the fall of 1801 contained no reference to the Louisiana problem. The President in that year had made every effort to maintain friendly ties with France even though it involved the acceptance of Bonaparte's conditions for the ratification of the Convention of 1800 and might require the reception of French envoys Laforest and Otto whom he considered to be anti-republican if not anti-American.

By 1802 the melancholy observations of Robert Livingston on France's imperial plans induced Jefferson to announce not only his knowledge of the Treaty of San Ildefonso but also his opposition to it. Pichon reported the change. Shortly after the President had assured the French Minister of his faith in France's disclaimers about Louisiana, he began to hint at a rupture between the two countries that would take place as soon as war was resumed in Europe. To avoid this state of affairs, Jefferson suggested that France provide Americans with favorable commercial concessions on the Mississippi. He had apparently decided to face the fact of French imperialism without waiting for French troops on American soil to rouse him to action.

The President's aim now was to persuade France by intimidation to give up her ambitions in America. The price of America's friendship would be more than economic favors from the new masters of Louisiana; France would have to cede New Orleans, the Floridas, all the territory that she received from Spain. If France should refuse his request, he predicted, she would lose the territory the moment the perennial troubles of Europe distracted her attention from the New World. France would be wiser to give up the land voluntarily and retain the good will of the United States. The alternative for Americans was an alliance with Britain. Dramatically, almost theatrically, Jefferson warned that "the day that France takes possession of N. Orleans, fixes the sentence which is to restrain her forever within her low-water mark. It seals the union of two nations, who in conjunction, can maintain exclusive possession of the ocean. From that moment we must marry ourselves to the British fleet and nation."

The President wrote these often quoted words in a letter to the American Minister to France for the beneficial effect he hoped they would have upon its bearer, Pierre Samuel Du Pont de Nemours, a distinguished physiocrat and a friend for almost twenty years. Although Du Pont was then a resident of the United States and was departing for France for what he thought would be only a brief stay, Jefferson saw an opportunity to exploit the economist's contacts with the French government by having him publicize the seriousness with which the United States regarded the Louisiana cession. Lest the Livingston letter fail in its purpose, the President sent Du Pont

a note in which he asked him to impress upon his fellow countrymen the importance of ceding all French territory in America, not
just New Orleans.

The unofficial emissary of America served faithfully the task which
Jefferson had chosen for him, but he did not accept it until his pride
as a Frenchman had been appeased. The President's tactics, he
thought, would antagonize rather than intimidate the French. It
would be better for the United States to help the French win Canada
in exchange for the surrender of Louisiana, for such a gesture would
permit the arrangement to appear reciprocal. If this plan were
impossible, he advised, Jefferson should offer a reasonable price for
the territory at issue, in language that would not offend Bonaparte.

While appreciating the spirit of friendship evidenced by Du
Pont's reply to his suggestion, the President was not at all pleased
with the idea of purchasing Louisiana. He had anticipated France's
compliance with his wishes on the strength of his threats and on the
hope of new conflicts in Europe. Only when his alternatives seemed
to be purchase or war did Jefferson turn to the Du Pont plan. The
world situation in general and his political fortunes in particular
allowed no other solution in 1802. Abroad, the Peace of Amiens had
been made in the very month in which he had made overtures to Du
Pont, and Rufus King reported that Britain, despite her interest in
the disposition of Louisiana, would not bring the Louisiana
question into her negotiations with France. Edward Thornton, the
British Chargé d'Affaires in Washington, even suggested that if the
French should occupy Louisiana, the British would have greater
influence over a frightened United States. Bonaparte was therefore
free to complete his plans for the occupation of the territory. At
home, the President had to contend with the rising anger of the
Westerners over the prospect of having their rights of deposit in
New Orleans taken away by the new rulers of the Mississippi.
Pinckney's Treaty with Spain in 1795 had given the United States
the right to navigate the Mississippi from its source to the sea, and
to deposit its goods at New Orleans for transhipment to ocean-
going vessels. Spain suspended this right in October, 1802, and
France was immediately blamed for the affront. Federalists were
able to use Western discontent to embarrass the administration by
demanding redress from France and posing as the new champions
of the West.

The President responded to these challenges by employing a
weapon that his predecessors had used successfully a few years

before: a special mission empowered to' settle a special problem.
He chose James Monroe to be Minister Plenipotentiary and Envoy
Extraordinary to France to help Livingston win Louisiana from the
French. Jay's mission in 1794 had postponed Republican attacks
until a treaty with Britain had been made; Monroe, a popular figure
in the 'West, might have the same success, not only in silencing the
Federalists but also in dampening the ardor of the West for war.
Jefferson authorized the two envoys to purchase New Orleans and
the Floridas alone for a price slightly less than what was finally
paid for the entire Louisiana territory, and to guarantee if necessary
the rest of the territory to the French. Should France appear hostile,
they were to open talks with the British about the possibility of
co-operating in a joint venture against French Louisiana.

Thus Jefferson seemed to have completed over a period of four
years the process of detaching himself from France by going beyond
the policy of isolation to consider a British alliance long advocated
by the Hamiltonians. Such an extreme course is characteristic of the
ex-revolutionary of every era, who, finding his love betrayed, will
seek any means to destroy the former object of his affections. The
President's behaviour, however, was not an emotional 'by-product
of hatred for France. At no time did he express personal anger
toward that country, or, conversely, extend a sincere welcome to
Britain as a defender of liberty. His flamboyant talk of a British
alliance was only a gambit of international politics in which he
hoped to use Britain to intimidate France, for he never seriously
considered an alliance with Britain as a real possibility. Britain
remained the traditional enemy in the eyes of the President and of
the Secretary of State, for whom Britain's ambitions in the West,
transgressions on the seas, and possible stipulations for the price
of support overbalanced the transitory threat of France.

Inasmuch as France never completed her empire in America,
there can be no certainty as to the extent to which Jefferson might
have gone to counter the moves of Bonaparte. During the difficult
days of 1802 his fears often dented the armor of confidence he had
built out of hopes that the troubles of the Old World would in some
way prove to be his salvation. On such occasions he would be convinced that France would force the United States into the arms of
Britain, and so he took pleasure in noting every manifestation of
friendship on the part of the British. But generally Jefferson's dally-
ing with Britain was so half-hearted and so palpably self-seeking
that Thornton, with whom he attempted to ingratiate himself in

gloomy moments, distrusted his sudden appreciation of British merits and claimed that he seemed to tax "his imagination to supply the deficiency of his feeling." Thornton was right. When Jefferson's mood of despair lifted, he trusted in the intervention of a *deus ex machina*—war in Europe, revolution in the West Indies, or financial difficulties in France—to make France see the light and to keep his country out of the clutches of Britain. Months before he had seen any of his hopes realized, the President railed against those Americans who would have the United States take immediate action on Louisiana. Nothing but dire necessity, he asserted, could force the country out of neutrality and into the orbit of Britain. And such a crisis looked distant as reports began coming in about the restoration of American rights of deposit in New Orleans, the imminence of war in Europe, and difficulties that Leclerc's French armies were having in occupying the island of Santo Domingo. The President's willingness to guarantee Louisiana to France as well as his talk of a British alliance must be weighed against his knowledge that the future of the territory irrevocably belonged to the rising West and against his conviction that British services should never be used to help obtain it.

When all Louisiana and not just New Orleans fell into the hands of the surprised envoys in May 1803, the event took place in the manner that Jefferson had predicted. Bonaparte had to sacrifice his imperial ambitions in the New World, temporarily at least, before the altar of a new war in Europe. Since British sea power would have prevented him from occupying his American empire, he deemed it advisable to sell the entire territory to the United States, despite the dubious legality of such a transaction, and receive in return funds to carry on his European ventures. Other explanations for the First Consul's actions are available. George Dangerfield has recently pointed out that failure in Santo Domingo made war in Europe inevitable: Bonaparte needed a new arena in which to recoup his losses. Whatever may have been the ultimate factor in the decision, Jefferson had a right to feel that he had won complete success. He had vindicated not only the policy of non-entanglement advocated by Washington and Adams but also the assumption he had made as Secretary of State: America's advantage from Europe's distress.

Although Jefferson from 1798 to 1803 appeared to have cut most of the bonds that had formerly linked his emotions and his activities favorably to the French nation, his experiences did not make him either a political or an ideological Franco-phobe. He did not wake up to French imperialism until the Directory had fallen, and when it finally made an impression upon him, it was associated with Bonaparte and not with the Revolution. With the Revolution destroyed, it seemed that Jefferson had forgotten his own vigorous championship of France a few years earlier. He bore no grudge against the people who betrayed his faith.

Jefferson the President had taken up the view of France he had held as Minister to that country, when he had urged cautious reform so that she might more effectively serve as a buffer protecting the United States from Britain. He was therefore disappointed but not particularly surprised or disturbed by the mere fact of a firm dictatorship. Whatever the government, French power could still serve the purposes of American policy as long as the United States did not allow itself to become involved in Bonaparte's European conflicts. Even the intrusion of the Louisiana issue did not basically affect Jefferson's interpretation of the balance of power which he had formulated years before. While Louisiana in French hands made France the chief threat to America in 1802, she was only a temporary menace to American sovereignty with which he could cope by trusting in Europe's propensity for wars and in his own skill in diplomacy. Britain, on the other hand, was a permanent and far more dangerous adversary. But for the moment, the contribution of the new Anglo-French war to the Louisiana Purchase permitted him to consider Britain and France each "as a necessary instrument to hold in check the disposition of the other to tyrannize over other nations."

PART TWO

The Coming of War

1 FROM   *A. L. Burt*
The United States, Great Britain and British North America

International law in the early nineteenth century was complicated and uncertain. It was complicated because it consisted of agreed-upon rules based on centuries of precedents, and it was uncertain because it was being constantly altered in the Napoleonic wars by the unilateral actions of the great powers. The United States was more affected by the actions of Great Britain, however, for Great Britain controlled the high seas after the battle of Trafalgar in 1805. Of all British actions, the most deeply felt and profoundly resented was impressment. To have American citizens forcibly taken from ships of the United States was an affront that most felt could not be tolerated. To have them seized by the very country whose rule had only been recently thrown off was doubly insulting. But, in addition to impressment, there was a variety of other disputes. These included arguments over the Rule of 1756, blockades, broken and continuous voyages, and the British Orders in Council. Each of these would have been sufficient to have strained to the near breaking point relations between Britain and America. Taken together, they were to prove fatal. The clearest discussion of these complicated issues is to be found in Professor A. L. Burt's study, The United States, Great Britain and British North America.

NEUTRAL RIGHTS

Impressment was the most baffling issue between the two countries. Though thrust forward by the war, it was not a question of the laws

SOURCE. A. L. Burt, *The United States, Great Britain and British North America* (New Haven: Yale University Press for the Carnegie Endowment for International Peace, 1940), pp. 211–224. Reprinted with the permission of the Carnegie Endowment for International peace and the author.

of war which define the balance between belligerent and neutral
rights. It concerned something more permanent, more deep-seated
—sovereignty. It was raised by the attraction of British seamen to
the American service. They deserted the navy, where life was too
much like a floating hell; and they left the British mercantile marine,
whence they were liable at any time to be impressed into the navy.
There was only one place where they could go, and it was an inviting
heaven where they would be at home right away. The merchant
marine of the United States was hungry for sailors. Under the
stimulus of the war, it was expanding so rapidly that it required four
or five thousand additional hands every year. The increased demand
tripled American wages afloat. This salvation of the British tar, however, threatened the destruction of Britain by draining the lifeblood
of her sea power, the one thing that stood between her and downfall. To check this vital loss, British warships searched American
vessels and removed British fugitives.

Necessity overrides law, and Britain was impelled by necessity.
But she insisted that her action was not illegal. Though this may
seem strange now, it was not then, for important developments in
international law and usage have since taken place. One is in our
concept of nationality. We have become accustomed to think of
people changing their national status almost as readily as they
change their shirts. Then nationality was commonly considered to
be about as impossible to change as one's skin. It is the phenomenal
growth of the United States by immigration that has made the
difference, and even yet the new American-born principle has not
gained universal acceptance. This principle, however, played no
part in the quarrel over impressment. The American government
did not pretend to throw the protecting cloak of American naturalization around the bodies of these British fugitives. The quarrel over
impressment turned on the right of search for deserters, and on the
abuses which inevitably accompanied the practice.

The right of search was the main point in the dispute, and here
the clash between the past and the future stands out clearly. The
British position rested on the prerogative of sovereignty to pursue
fugitive nationals anywhere up to a line where another sovereignty
barred the pursuit. The United States claimed no right to protect
American vessels from search in British territorial waters; nor, on
the other hand, did Britain claim the right of search within territorial waters of the United States. It was a question of jurisdiction
on the high seas, over which there was of course no sovereignty, and

there the difference was not over the immunity of government vessels. Though the *Chesapeake* incident has at times led people to suppose the contrary, Britain never asserted the right to search units of the United States Navy. What she did assert, and the United States deny, was the right to search private vessels because this involved no invasion of another sovereignty. Both sides were right, Britain by the old usage, and the United States by a new doctrine then only beginning to take shape: that a country's ships at sea are detached portions of its soil and therefore covered by its sovereignty. Though already admitted for public vessels, it was not yet really established for private ones. Even today this sovereignty is not as complete as that which exists on land or within the limits of territorial waters, and the United States admitted qualification then. The American government recognized, for example, the British right to stop and search private American ships for contraband in time of war.

It was the abuses which accompanied the practice of searching for deserters that inflamed the quarrel, and these abuses occurred on both sides. The British never claimed the right to impress American seamen, but they did impress them as British subjects. It was often impossible to tell the difference between the American and the British members of a crew, for there was no national distinction of language, physical appearance, dress, or manners. British deserters sailing under the Stars and Stripes would insist that they belonged to that flag; and the officers under whom they were serving, loath to lose valuable hands, would support their contention. A boarding officer in search of men whom he badly needed was judge in his own cause, and there was no real check upon his arbitrary decisions. No officer who seized goods as contraband could touch his share of the prize until it was brought into port and there condemned after a legal trial of the seizure, but there was no such procedure to protect human beings seized on the wide ocean. The only way to rescue an American thus carried off was to prove to the Admiralty that he was an American, and then an order for his release would be issued; but this was a difficult business and painfully slow. Early in the first period of the war the American government thought to check the abuse by what were known as "protections." These were certificates of American citizenship issued by magistrates at home and consuls abroad. But the granting of these papers was not hedged about by proper restrictions. It was all too easy for a British tar to get one. They were often given out indiscriminately; sailors lost them and sold them; they were cheap. So notorious did the traffic become that the device made things worse instead of better. British officers naturally came to have nothing but scorn for these official documents of the United States. As the years passed, the number of kidnapped Americans serving in the Royal Navy mounted until it was several thousand. This right of search and practice of impressment was the British counterpart of the unrestricted submarine campaign conducted by Germany a century later, for it touched American lives, and lives are more precious than goods.

Interference with American trade, the other great issue which the French war raised between the United States and Britain, was a complicated question. Though some references have previously been made to this problem, a fuller analysis is necessary here. The trouble springs from the very nature of war. It is a triangular affair. In addition to the clash of arms between belligerents, it precipitates a clash of interest between belligerent and neutral over intercourse with the enemy. The one would like to stop it completely and the other to continue it without any interruption. Long experience has tended to work out a rough compromise between them, for both have felt the restraint of prudence, the belligerent fearing to push the neutral to the point of open hostility, and the neutral shrinking from resistance that would mean fighting. Hence it came to be generally recognized that a belligerent could seize and condemn as legal prize any neutral vessel and cargo containing contraband being sent to the enemy country; and also, under the same penalty, could prohibit any neutral vessel, no matter what her cargo, from entering or leaving a blockaded port of the enemy.

All governments admitted that arms and accouterments of war constituted contraband, but there was no common agreement upon the further definition of the term. The textbook writers offered confusing advice. From the conflicting precedents which they recorded, they could deduce only the general principle that other things which might be used by the fighting forces could be treated as contraband when particular circumstances warranted such procedure. A few treaties gave greater precision to the meaning of the word; but there was conflict between them, and each had only a limited application. Thus the original clash of interest survived. Belligerents sought to expand the definition of the term, and neutrals to contract it. Both dressed up selfish interests as legal rights, and the decision between them was left as before to force tempered by prudence. Because the British soon chased the French from the sea, it was the interest of the latter to uphold the narrowest neutral view, and of the former to maintain the opposite, so that over this question the United States became embroiled with Britain and not with France. As we have already seen, however, prudential considerations moved Britain to qualify her seizure of provisions as contraband by purchasing them and paying demurrage. But this was only a mitigation of a principle which Americans regarded as evil; and when France and the United States made up their quarrel in 1800, Bonaparte apparently tried to revive the Anglo-American quarrel over the principle by inserting in his treaty with the United States a definition of contraband as warlike material only.

More exasperating difficulties grew out of the application of the other principle mentioned above. When was a blockade not a blockade ? It was commonly conceded that a blockade had to be officially declared and had to be effective, but there was absolutely no consensus of opinion on what was "effective." Here treaties and classical authorities were of much less assistance than in the definition of contraband. Here Nature intervened to render impossible the formulation of any but a very general rule when it was at last adopted by the principal powers, with the exception of the United States, in the Declaration of Paris in 1856. So variable was the combination of such essential conditions as channels, currents, coasts, and weather, that each application of a blockade was a special problem. Here also Bonaparte tried to feed the starved Anglo-American quarrel by inserting into his treaty of 1800 a narrow definition of blockade. As long as the problem of blockade was confined to single ports, it was relatively simple; but, as will be noticed presently, that limitation soon disappeared in the titanic struggle between Britain and the Napoleonic Empire, and it has never returned.

From the ancient and undoubted right of a belligerent to capture private ships and goods of the enemy at sea, sprang other issues between the United States and Britain. One was the principle of "free ships, free goods," which would limit this right by giving immunity to enemy goods, other than contraband, on board neutral vessels. The limitation was so severe that, if enforced, it would have largely destroyed the value of the right, for an enemy could then trade with impunity under the protection of neutral flags. It was a doctrine made by neutrals in the interest of neutrals, to whom it would hand over the carrying trade of belligerents. Its advocates gave it a specious appearance of justice by coupling it with the converse, "enemy ships, enemy goods," which would likewise benefit neutrals by discouraging neutral use of belligerent bottoms. Free ships, free goods, was another of the principles laid down in the Declaration of Paris in 1856. At the time of the French Revolutionary wars, it was a subject of rather violent disagreement. It was already well on the way to establishment, for it had been written into a number of specific treaties. Even Britain had signed an odd treaty embodying it, but she had never admitted its general application, and she could not do so then without playing into the hands of France. For this very reason, France had lined up with the neutral powers; and she tried to use them, particularly her American protégé and ally, in forcing it upon Britain. It was the official doctrine of the United States government, but opinion in the country was far from being unanimous in support of it. When Jefferson was Secretary of State, he wrote to Genet: "It cannot be doubted, but that, by the general law of nations, the goods of a friend found in the vessel of an enemy are free, and the goods of an enemy found in the vessel of a friend are lawful prize." Jay's failure to insert the principle in his treaty was to the French a violation of their treaty with the United States signed in 1778, and therefore one of the grounds of the subsequent Franco-American breach. In repairing this, Bonaparte revived the subtle French game. One of the maritime principles which he put into his treaty of September, 1800, with the United States was "free ships, free goods."

Of more serious consequence was the disputed right of neutrals in time of war to enter a trade that was shut to them in time of peace. This likewise threatened to destroy the value of the belligerent right to capture enemy property at sea. No compromise principle of any kind had arisen to regulate this issue. It involved two important branches of trade—coasting and colonial. Both were almost universally preserved as strict national monopolies in the period with which we are concerned. If a belligerent, exercising the clear right of capturing enemy ships and cargoes, could drive the enemy from the sea, the enemy would naturally seek relief by temporarily opening its monopoly to neutrals. If they took advantage of this indulgence they would certainly be bringing succor to the distressed enemy. Could neutrals do it and yet remain neutrals?

It was the colonial side of the question which first thrust itself forward, and therefore the first to get any answer. That was in the Seven Years' War, during which the British Empire devoured most of the French Empire overseas. Hard pressed by British maritime superiority, France was unable to supply her West Indies or to bring their produce to Europe under her own flag; and therefore she resorted to the expedient of relaxing her colonial monopoly in favor of neutrals. To counter this novel action, the British prize courts promulgated the novel doctrine which came to be known as "the Rule of the War of 1756," and later simply "the Rule of 1756," to which reference has already been made in a previous chapter. It was naturally a categorical negative to the question just stated. Made in Britain to support the interest of Britain, it was another illustration of law being the declared will of superior force. But there was justice in the contention that a trade prohibited by municipal law during peace should be prohibited by international law during war. It deprived neutrals of no right which they enjoyed prior to the outbreak of war, and it was necessary to preserve the value of an unquestioned belligerent right. It was a new rule called forth by new conditions, and it was promulgated in the only way possible. Yet, however just it might be, it ran counter to the interests of neutrals and of belligerents that suffered from naval impotence; and they would not recognize the validity of this fiat of a single power.

The first American collision with this rule, as we have already seen, nearly precipitated the United States into a declaration of war in the spring of 1794. Indeed Britain had overstepped her own mark by ordering the indiscriminate capture of American vessels trafficking in the French West Indies, for a limited trade in American vessels of small burthen had been legalized before the war; and she drew back just in time. She then contented herself with only a partial application of the rule, ordering the capture of vessels laden in the French West Indies with produce of those islands and sailing thence for Europe. The fruits of the naval superiority of the belligerent were being shared with a neutral.

The nature of this compromise is worth noting. It was confined to a single neutral, the United States, and it was wholly practical. Britain did not renounce any part of her full right under the Rule of 1756. What she did was done voluntarily, under no pressure from America, for the restrained practice was inaugurated long before people in the United States knew that the unrestrained practice had begun. When Jay went to London he found it impossible to extract a renunciation of the principle, as desired by his government. So intent were the British on retaining it that they persuaded him to accept a provision which, without formally according any recognition of the principle, would throw a legal cloak over the practical compromise until two years after the war ended. This was the price exacted for the opening of the much coveted British West Indian trade to American shipping during the same period. The bargain was made in Article XII of the treaty, which bound the American government to make it illegal for American bottoms to carry molasses, sugar, coffee, cocoa, or cotton anywhere except to the United States. These, of course, were the staples of the island colonies; and the object of this provision was to limit American intercourse with the West Indies, both British and French, to a direct trade. American ships were to be forbidden to supply Europe with any such produce even if it had first been landed in the United States. This article would have given an American guarantee, not only to the British monopoly of the transatlantic trade with British colonies, but also to the British prohibition of the same trade with French colonies under the Rule of 1756. The Senate rejected this article because it would outlaw a lawful and profitable American commerce between the French West Indies and France via the United States, recent decisions of British prize courts having legitimized it under the doctrine of the "broken voyage." The Senate's action saved the United States from winking at the Rule of 1756, so that the nature of the compromise remained untouched. It continued to be a matter solely of British grace inspired by prudence.

The liberality of this compromise, and its adoption by unilateral action, may seem to imply a tacit admission on the part of Britain that the principle she had enunciated to meet new conditions in the Seven Years' War did not apply to the yet newer conditions created by American independence, and therefore should not be applied against the United States. The late Admiral Mahan was inclined to draw this deduction, but it is not quite just. This particular British moderation was simply part and parcel of the regular British policy to keep the interference of belligerent rights with neutral rights down to the minimum necessitated by the exigencies of war. In this instance the interference was considerably less than landlubbers might imagine, for the trade winds blew away much of the hardship imposed on American vessels. They did not have to go very far out of their regular course to call at an American port when sailing from the West Indies to Europe. Yet the situation was fraught with danger. In the American treaty of reconciliation with France in 1800, Bonaparte committed the United States to a definition of commercial rights which condemned the British principle without naming it. But he could not rouse the American government over this issue. Only Britain could do that. The danger lay in the nature of the compromise. At any time the British prize courts might shift the basis of their rulings, substituting the "continuous" for the "broken" voyage, and the British government might decide to apply the Rule of 1756 in all its rigor. This decision was never made, but the shift did occur, upsetting the compromise and precipitating trouble.

American action, both public and private, was responsible for destroying the foundation of the British prize-court decisions favorable to the American interest. The doctrine of the broken voyage rested on the assumption that the goods in question were legally imported for use in the United States before they were reëxported. Importation meant the payment of customs duties, and the performance of such operations as unloading, checking, weighing, and storing, all of which involved time and expense. The corresponding operations attendant upon exportation of course added more to the cost. Here were hardships which the trade winds could not blow away, but American ingenuity might remove. . . .

Whether neutrals could engage in the coasting trade of an enemy —the other part of the question which had evoked the Rule of 1756—remained in the background much longer than the problem of colonial trade. Though it had not yet pressed for an answer, Bonaparte's treaty with the United States in 1800 supplied one inferentially. The definition of commercial rights mentioned above stipulated the freedom of a neutral to navigate between enemy ports. Not until some little time after the renewal of hostilities in 1803 did the issue thrust itself forward, and then it was soon obscured by other issues. As Napoleon's power spread on land and Britain's grew on the sea, he was relieved and she was frustrated by neutrals' taking over the coasting trade of his empire. Sooner or later she was bound to strike at their interference in this new sphere as she had struck at their interference in colonial trade during the Seven Years' War. She held her hand until January, 1807, when, finding a plausible excuse in Napoleon's recent Berlin Decree which was still little more than an empty threat, she outlawed all commerce between ports under his control. Apparently this extension of the Rule of 1756 was directed at northern Europeans, chiefly the Danes, rather than the Americans, but it was plainly recognized that they would feel the blow too. The American government promptly protested that the British action was illegal unless based on "actual blockades," and pointed out that it would ruin a trade which Britain herself recognized as wholly legitimate. The profits of a voyage com-

monly depended on dropping some cargo here and some there, and
on picking up a return cargo in the same way. If an American
merchantman had to make the whole exchange in one place, it
might as well not go to France at all.

Thus did the issue over the enemy's coasting trade come into the
open when the issue over the enemy's colonial trade was finally
chased out of its hole by the doctrine of the continuous voyage.
Together they were capable of doing great damage to Anglo-
American relations, and therefore it is easy to imagine the havoc
wrought by the quarrel which soon swallowed them up along with
all the other particular issues concerning trade—the quarrel over
Napoleon's Berlin and Milan decrees and Britain's equally famous
orders-in-council.

To understand these decrees and orders, we should remember
that they accompanied the approach of the supreme crisis in the
life-and-death struggle between the two powers which were then by
far the greatest on earth. Napoleon had come to realize that his
position in Europe would never be secure until he subdued Britain,
and she that her freedom depended on his downfall. Having had to
abandon his projected invasion of the island kingdom because
British sea power effectively barred the way, he perforce fell back
upon the use of his land power to accomplish by slow strangulation
what was impossible by quick assault. Taking advantage of the fact
that Britain had stretched her declaration of blockade to cover a
considerable length of his northern coast line, he stretched his
declaration still farther and justified his action as a proper reprisal.
He proclaimed the blockade of the whole of the British Isles.

This was a sort of fantastic and inverted blockade. Napoleon had
no navy to enforce it, and his object was not so much to keep goods
from reaching Britain as it was to prevent them from leaving.
Because of this inversion, however, and also because of the wide
extent of his power upon the Continent, he could undertake to
enforce the blockade without a navy. This was what he was doing
when he ordered the confiscation of all British goods and also,
under pain of confiscation, the exclusion of every ship that touched
at a British port. By depriving Britain of access to the European
market upon which her economic life depended, he calculated that
he could soon reduce the nation of traders and manufacturers to cry
for mercy. Such, in short, was his Continental System which he
began to enforce vigorously in the late summer of 1807. Britain saw
that, if he carried it through, she was done. The orders-in-council

were her desperate reply. She extended her blockade to every port from which he excluded her ships; and she turned back upon him the provisions of his own decrees, declaring that she would treat as an enemy any ship which, without first going to Britain, sought to enter any port controlled by him.

The position of neutrals became impossible. It would have been much easier for them if they could have chosen to trade either with Britain or with the Napoleonic empire, but this was not the alternative that was forced upon them. The real issue was the Continental System. Would they coöperate with Napoleon in upholding it, or with Britain in undermining it? The question presented a perfect dilemma. A neutral vessel could not approach any European port that was under Napoleon's sway without being liable to seizure, either outside by a ship of the Royal Navy or inside by Napoleon's officials; inside, if it had touched at a British port, or had procured British papers; outside, if it had not. It was a choice between the devil and the deep sea.

Each belligerent was coercing neutrals to serve its own end; and as neutral rights disappeared under the combined pressure, each belligerent defended its departures from the traditional law of nations by accusing the other of prior violations and by blaming neutrals for their non-resistance to these violations. Neutrals, however, could not accept the self-justification of either without shedding their neutrality, nor could they offer resistance to either without running the same risk. Resistance to both was unthinkable. It was then more terribly true than ever that law is what those who can and will enforce it say that it is; and that the principle of reprisal, once let loose, may destroy the other principles of the laws of war. Indeed, the "laws of war" is a contradiction in terms.

Both belligerents this time flouted the United States, and both professed eagerness to resume conformity to traditional law; but each insisted that the other should do it first, or that the Americans should resist with force the coercion of the other. Theoretically, the two belligerents were equally oppressive; but practically, legally, and psychologically they were not. Britain's control of the sea, being greater than Napoleon's control of the land, gave her greater power of enforcement. Much more important was the legal difference. Her seizures were made at sea and therefore, according to her own admission, were a violation of neutral rights under international law, her justification being that it was a necessary reprisal against Napoleon. His seizures, except an occasional capture by a fugitive

French frigate or privateer at sea, were all made in port and therefore within the undoubted jurisdiction of his own or a subordinate
government. Strictly speaking, his only violation of neutral rights
under international law was confined to the occasional captures just
mentioned. Napoleon also struck a responsive chord in the United
States when he denounced the orders-in-council as designed to
establish the economic supremacy of England upon the ruins of the
industry and commerce of European countries. Here we approach
another fundamental factor in the growing Anglo-American
bitterness.

Between Britain and the United States there was a mutual
suspicion mounting to a settled conviction that each was using the
war to cheat the other out of its rights. The British were exasperated
by the paradox of their position. Never had they possessed such
complete control of the sea, yet more than ever the sea-borne trade
of the enemy was escaping from their grasp. As already suggested,
neutrals were running off with it and giving it their protection.
They were climbing up on the back of the British navy, whose
supremacy persuaded the enemy to hand over this trade; and they
were throwing dust in the eyes of British judges, causing them to
release as neutral what was really enemy property. By such means
not only were they expanding their merchant marine while that of
Britain shrank; they were actually robbing her of the profitable
prizes of war and also of the crowning prize of a victorious end to
the war. In other words, their cupidity had leagued them with the
enemy and drawn them into an underhand war against Britain. The
tricks by which they performed the daily miracle of transforming
enemy into neutral commerce were publicly exposed, and a new
British policy was demanded, by James Stephen in his *War in
Disguise, or the Frauds of the Neutral Flags*, a pamphlet of more than
two hundred pages which appeared in the fall of 1805. The author
knew whereof he spoke, for he was perhaps the leading practitioner
in the prize appeal court and he had earlier followed his profession
in the West Indies. He probably shared the responsibility for the
adoption of the principle of the continuous voyage, but this did not
satisfy him. He was positive that there was only one cure for the
evil, and that was a rigorous application of the Rule of 1756. Even
if it drove neutrals into open hostilities, that would be preferable
to this covert war. Britain would then be free to use her strength to
strike down those who were injuring her.

Stephen gave forceful expression to a latent but growing feeling of hostility against neutrals in general and Americans in particular. It was directed against Americans in particular because they were gathering by far the greatest harvest at British ·expense, their mercantile marine having rapidly become the only great rival of Britain's. The pamphlet was very popular, running through three editions in four months. It undoubtedly had a great effect upon public opinion and may even have had some part, as has been supposed, in suggesting the famous orders-in-council. Be this as it may, the chief significance of Stephen's outburst would appear to have been symptomatic rather than causal. The logic of events was teaching Britain that she could not much longer allow neutrals to reap where she had sown.

As British people believed that Americans were abusing their neutral rights to the vital injury of Britain, so were Americans convinced that Britain was abusing her temporary belligerent rights to serve her permanent economic interests and that in doing so she was furtively dealing a dangerous blow at their country. They saw her trying, under cover of the war, to monopolize the commerce of the world. This may seem absurd when we remember that their mercantile marine had enjoyed a phenomenal expansion through the war while hers had suffered a contraction; but we should not overlook some other important considerations. Britain was in a position to do this very thing, international law being what it was and the Royal Navy being virtually supreme upon the sea; and there was no gainsaying the fact that measures which she took to win the war also tended to benefit her own carrying trade and commerce at the expense of others. In the United States this further effect was bound to be regarded as intentional and not just incidental. The adoption of the doctrine of the continuous voyage contained the suggestion that Britain would destroy what she could not appropriate; and the orders-in-council seemed to prove it.

The American reaction appears all the more natural when viewed in the light of the past. Britain had laid herself open to this suspicion by a policy which she, and she alone, had followed for generations. It was the policy of her navigation laws, by which she excluded foreigners from all but a corner of her carrying trade. This application of the monopolistic principle was purposely made to stimulate the growth of the country's merchant marine, and was commonly credited, both at home and abroad, with having made it what it was—the greatest in the world. Another object of the exclusion of foreigners was to deprive them, particularly the Dutch, of their function as middlemen in international trade, and to transfer this function and its profits to England. Not unconsciously had she become the chief storehouse and clearinghouse of the world's commerce, or, to use the language of the day, the great entrepot. She had attained a position where she held the world in fee. It is not surprising, therefore, that non-British eyes saw in the orders-in-council a new and ruthless projection of the old and selfish design. To Americans, of all people, these orders-in-council were particularly offensive. The reason for their peculiar sensitiveness lay in their own history; they were being forced back into the dependence of colonial days. Once more Britain was insisting that they should have no trade of their own, that all their foreign commerce must be under her control. American Independence was at stake!

2 FROM *Reginald Horsman*
The Causes of the War of 1812

The United States came close to the brink of war in 1807. In that year the Chesapeake, *an American frigate on a shakedown cruise, was stopped by the British frigate* Leopard *whose commander demanded the surrender from it of a group of alleged British deserters. When this quite improper demand was rejected, the British first fired on the* Chesapeake *and then boarded the vessel to seize the men involved. The reaction in the United States was predictable. Calls for war rang throughout the country. Certainly the affront to the United States was unprecedented. One of her naval vessels had been wantonly attacked and members of her crew killed or wounded. It is true that Britain was quick to apologize and to disclaim any right to stop and search a public vessel of another nation.*

But an apology without the cessation of impressment was not sufficient for Jefferson. Was war then the only honorable alternative? Again, Jefferson did not think so. The nation was not armed for it, and the President was certain that other measures could be taken which would force Britain to change her conduct. And so he proposed an embargo. After quick cabinet discussion the measure was rushed through Congress. It provided for a total embargo on the shipment of American goods overseas. Its effectiveness was suspect from the beginning, and it was finally repealed in 1809. Professor Reginald Horsman in his Causes of the War of 1812 *gives an effective and thorough analysis of both events.*

THE *CHESAPEAKE* AFFAIR AND THE EMBARGO

The danger to peace was nearer than Madison realized, and it came from a source that only serves to emphasize that between 1803 and 1807 it was impressment, more than any other factor, that was responsible for the sharp decline in Anglo-American relations. In the early months of 1807, a British squadron was lying at anchor in Chesapeake Bay waiting for the appearance of two French ships that had taken refuge in United States waters. While there, the British obtained water and supplies from the mainland, and this presented an opportunity for British sailors to desert. Several took the opportunity to do so, and the matter reached a crisis on March 7

SOURCE. Reginald Horsman, *The Causes of the War of 1812* (Philadelphia: University of Pennsylvania Press, 1962), pp. 102–112. Copyright © by the Trustees of the University of Pennsylvania. Used by permission.

69

when a boat's crew of British seamen escaped and rowed to shore. Many of them joined American ships, including several who enlisted on board the American frigate *Chesapeake* and flaunted their new-found freedom in the streets of Norfolk. The British officers appealed for them without success, and then reported their grievances to the British commander-in-chief at Halifax, Vice-Admiral George C. Berkeley. Berkeley, angry at this flouting of British power, issued an order to the ships of his command that should they meet the *Chesapeake* at sea they were to search her for deserters. On June 22, 1807, the *Chesapeake* weighed anchor and put out to sea. When she was only eight or nine miles off shore she was approached by the British ship *Leopard*, and a man was sent on board to request the handing over of deserters. Commander Barron of the *Chesapeake* refused this request, and the British ship fired first across the bows of the American vessel and then directly into her, killing three and wounding eighteen. The American vessel was forced to strike her colors, and the British searched her and took off four men.

The return of the *Chesapeake* to Hampton Roads produced a sensation which almost drove America into open hostility against England. The whole country cried for war with a revolutionary fervor. Augustus Foster, the British Secretary of Legation, was in the region of New York when he heard of the incident. Judging discretion to be the better part of valor, he immediately decided to travel incognito and entrusted his curricle and horses to the separate care of his groom. This proved a sound decision, as only the presence of a somewhat timid soul counseling moderation prevented the curricle and horses from being thrown into the North River. Foster revealed more than the temper of the American populace when he commented that "the ringleader on this occasion was, as might be expected, an Irish emigrant." New York's anger was paralleled throughout the country. At Norfolk a crowd destroyed the water casks of the British squadron, and the town administration forbade communication with the British ships in the bay. Even in New England, public meetings were held to denounce this latest attack on American shipping. It seemed that the injuries inflicted on America at sea between 1803 and 1807 had reached their culmination, and would at last bring open warfare.

Thomas Barclay, the British consul general in New York, wrote to George Canning on July 2 and stated that "the lower order of the Americans are much irritated and inclined for violent measures."

Elbridge Gerry of Massachusetts well expressed the national sentiment. "The public indignation is universally excited by the repeated
destruction of our unoffending seamen," he wrote, "if redress for
the present, and prevention for the future, cannot be obtained, will
not a state of warfare, be preferable to such a state of national
insult and degradation." This feeling continued throughout July,
and at the end of the month Erskine informed Canning that the
public excitement had still not subsided. America was ripe for war.

Jefferson's first reaction was to issue a proclamation on
July 2 expelling all armed British ships from American waters. Yet
in this moment of great crisis, the President maintained his calm
and good sense. At a time when he so easily could have had war, he
kept the peace. On June 29 he wrote to the governor of Virginia,
saying that the decision as to whether the outrage should be
answered by war rested with Congress, and that the cabinet should
do nothing to commit that body. His own sentiments were
expressed quite plainly by his argument that this "will leave
Congress free to decide whether war is the most efficacious mode
of redress in our case, or whether, having taught so many other
useful lessons to Europe, we may not add that of showing them that
there are peaceable means of redressing injustice, by making it the
interest of the aggressor to do what is just, and abstain from future
wrong." Jefferson, for all his talk of war with Spain, believed
essentially in achieving his ends through peaceful means. He wrote
on July 9 that "both reason & the usage of nations" required that
America should give Britain time to disavow the acts of her officers,
and that this would also give America time to bring home her
property, vessels, and seamen—"the only means of carrying on the
kind of war we should attempt." If war came he wanted only
limited fighting, and he leaned toward the idea that nonintercourse
was preferable to war. War, if absolutely necessary, could be fought
by privateers.

The measures taken by Jefferson were calculated to use time to
assuage the temper of the country rather than to take advantage
of it to produce war. At a cabinet meeting at the beginning of July,
it was decided to send the *Revenge* to England to demand satisfaction
for the attack on the *Chesapeake*. It was also agreed that Congress
would not be called until October. This measure obviously gave
time for the ardor of opinion to cool. Jefferson argued that the
three months before the convening of Congress would give time for
the *Revenge* to go to England and return with the answer—"Con-

gress would not declare war without a demand of satisfaction, nor
could they lay an Embargo with so much under the grasp of our
adversary." Madison's instructions to Monroe asked for disavowal
of the act, for reparations, and for the restoration of the four
seamen. Unfortunately, he also asked that this should be accompanied by an entire abolition of impressments. This was to leave
the *Chesapeake* incident as a running sore for four years, as Britain
quite obviously was not prepared to connect the two matters.
Reparation for the attack would have been distinctly possible.
England, as Canning re-emphasized in a letter to Monroe on
August 3, had never claimed the right to impress from American
warships, but to give up *all* impressment was impossible for any
British Government.

In the middle of July, when the *Revenge* set sail for England,
America would have followed Jefferson into war. "The public mind
is settling itself every where into a determined stand at the present
crisis," wrote Madison, "the Proclamation is rallied to by all parties.
Reparation or war is proclaimed at every meeting, or rather by every
mouth, which is not British." Jacob Crowinshield, the influential
New England Republican, wrote from Salem that there would be no
considerable opposition to any measure of retaliation, and that the
New England states would support the administration in any system
calculated to give effect to its just demands for reparation. Even
the cautious Albert Gallatin at first wanted war, and thought that it
was inevitable. In July he quickly produced a plan for financing the
coming war and presented it to Jefferson. Yet writing from New
York in the middle of August, he expressed the view that "the
people of this city do not appear to me to be in favor of war, and
they fear it so much that they have persuaded themselves that there
is no danger of that event." This view was substantially in agreement
with that of the British consul general in New York, Thomas
Barclay. He expressed the opinion that the New England states, and
the great proportion of the "respectable characters" in his own
state of New York, were averse to war with Great Britain. He considered, however, that as one progressed southward opinions
against Great Britain became warmer until in Maryland, Virginia,
and the Carolinas he thought that war would be a popular measure.
It would seem that though some observers were inclined to disagree
with the Republican Crowinshield's view that Federalist New
England would support the war, or that commercial New York
would give it full support, President Jefferson would have gained

considerable popular support if he had decided on war in the summer of 1807.

Vice-Admiral Berkeley, whose order had produced all this agitation, showed little repentance for his action and gave a glimpse of
naval attitudes in a letter to Earl Bathurst in the middle of August.
He expressed the view that it was most unlikely that hostilities could
be avoided, and that England needed force to awe the Americans,
if not to fight. His comment on the American scene, which was
described more with venom than with accuracy, was that "the
violence of the American rabble still continues, and as it accords
with the views of Jefferson and his party, it is not checked by
Government, but is kept up by every means in the numerous newspapers which are published."

In actual fact Jefferson was doing very little to take advantage of
the war feeling in the country. Throughout the summer of 1807 the
American government waited patiently for the return of the *Revenge*
from England. Patience had been a steady characteristic of American diplomacy in the period from the spring of 1806 to the summer
of 1807. For the greater part of these months America had waited
for a British answer to American proposals. The Non-Importation
Act, originally passed in April, 1806, had been delayed for practically a year, to wait the news of the Monroe-Pinkney Treaty. And even
after the bad news of that treaty had arrived, there had been a
further delay as Jefferson and Madison had tried to salvage the
doomed agreement. Now the *Chesapeake* affair was absorbing American opinion, and once again America settled down to await news
from England. Jefferson and Madison still hoped to avoid war, and
avoid it they did.

Jefferson, like so many of the early and some more recent
American statesmen, hoped that the complications of European
affairs would be America's salvation. He wrote on August 21, 1807,
that he had never thought that he would be under the necessity of
wishing success to Bonaparte, but as the English were as tyrannical
on the sea as the French were on the land, he felt obliged to say
"'down with England,' and as for what Bonaparte is then to do to
us, let us trust to the chapter of accidents. I cannot, with the
Anglomen, prefer a certain present evil to a future hypothetical
one.'" His argument was similar to that used by the British statesmen when they said that impressment might produce a war with
America, but better that more distant and problematical evil than
the certainty of defeat by Napoleon if there were no seamen to man

the ships. In fact, the wonder is not that England and America went to war in 1812, but that they avoided it for so long. To Jefferson, more than to any other individual, can this avoidance of war be attributed. If he had desired war, he could have had it in 1807.

Jefferson, anxious for peace, waited apprehensively for the return of the *Revenge* in the fall of 1807. He feared that war might well come, as he thought it very unlikely that England would agree to yield any of her maritime pretensions. Writing to Thomas Paine on October 9, he uttered a heart cry: "If they would but settle the question of impressment from our bottoms, I should be well contented to drop all attempts at a treaty. The other rights of neutral powers will be taken care of by Bonaparte and Alexander, and for commercial arrangements we can sufficiently provide by legislative regulations, but as the practice of impressment has taken place only against us we shall be left to settle that for ourselves. And to do this we shall never again have so favourable a conjuncture of circumstances." The importance of impressment in bringing England and America to the brink of war in the summer of 1807 was rarely, if at all, more emphatically stated than in this letter to Paine. Gallatin, however, now reluctant to commit America to a policy for which she was ill-prepared, urged caution even to the cautious Jefferson. He thought that the message Jefferson proposed to submit to Congress was too much like a manifesto against Great Britain, and that if there was a chance of accommodation, America should not ruin it. Gallatin argued that the government would obtain general support if it went to war because England refused satisfaction in the *Chesapeake* affair, but not if it went to war because of England's refusal to make the proposed arrangement regarding impressment. In the latter case, Gallatin thought that measures short of actual hostilities might become proper, leaving to England the choice of war. He made the exceedingly relevant point that America's preparations for war were meager, and that if there was immediate war America might not even be able to protect New York.

On October 26, the day Congress assembled, Jefferson perhaps reflected his own attitude in describing the opinions of Congress. He said that the members, as far as he could judge, were extremely disposed for peace, "and as there is no doubt Great Britain will disavow the act of the Leopard, I am inclined to believe they will be more disposed to combat her practice of impressment by a non-importation law than by arms." Jefferson's sympathy for this plan of action had been well illustrated in his numerous references to the possibility of nonimportation and nonintercourse in his letters since the *Chesapeake* incident. On November 1 he added that "here we are pacifically inclined, if anything comes which will permit us to follow our inclinations." By November 30 he was asserting that an embargo was the most likely action that Congress would take, though the choice lay between "War, Embargo or Nothing." At that time news arrived from England that Canning had refused to link the *Chesapeake* affair with an agreement on impressment, but that he was about to send a special envoy to America to settle the former issue.

The situation seemed desperate, and on December 14 the long postponed Non-Importation Act at last went into operation against Great Britain. Yet worse was to come, for no sooner was the Non-Importation Act in force than news arrived from Great Britain that on October 17 England had made a strong reassertion of her right of impressment. On that date a proclamation had been issued recalling all British seamen from the service of foreign nations, and ordering British officers to seize such men found serving on foreign merchant vessels. It asserted that no grant of citizenship from a foreign nation discharged British seamen from their obligation to England. This was nothing novel—Britain had consistently maintained this position—but coming when it did, it showed the United States quite plainly that the Tory government, in spite of such incidents as that of the *Chesapeake*, was determined to impress from American merchant ships to the full extent of its ability.

As if this were not enough, news arrived almost simultaneously from Paris that Napoleon, now in complete command of the Continent, had started to enforce his Berlin Decree of December, 1806, against American commerce. This year of 1807 had seen Napoleon consolidate his gains of the previous year and advance to new victories. In June he had faced the Russians at Friedland and had overwhelmed them. Napoleon could now make peace on his own terms. Later in the month the French Emperor and the Russian Czar Alexander met on a raft on the Niemen, and on July 7 a formal treaty was concluded at Tilsit. Russia was to join in Napoleon's plan to exclude British trade from the Continent, and as the leading commercial neutral America could expect to suffer still more from the European belligerents. America's cup of misery was full, and indeed running over, when in the middle of December strong unofficial information arrived from England that she was going to place fresh restrictions upon American commerce. Official news of Britain's new Orders in Council was not to reach America for several weeks, but the new British reassertion of her impressment policy, combined with the enforcement of the French Berlin Decree and the expectation of a stricter British policy toward neutral trade, were enough to persuade Jefferson that the time had come for the total interdiction of the American trade to the outside world.

On December 17 Jefferson met with the cabinet and suggested an embargo which would coerce the European powers by preventing American shipping from sailing for foreign ports. The cabinet gave Jefferson its support, though on the following day Gallatin expressed doubts on the wisdom of the measure and argued that it would not produce a more moderate policy from Great Britain. Yet it was decided to send a special message to Congress, and after a morning meeting of the cabinet a communication drafted by Madison reached the Senate on the afternoon of December 18. It told of the danger to American vessels, seamen, and merchandise, and asked Congress to consider the total prohibition of the departure of vessels from the ports of the United States. The Senate acted with great rapidity, referring the message to a committee and passing an Embargo Bill by a vote of 22 to 6 on the same afternoon that it received the President's message. The bill, which confined American vessels to American ports and permitted foreign vessels to leave only in ballast or with cargo they already had on board, was immediately sent to the House. It there passed by a vote of 82 to 44 after two days' debate. Congress had concurred in Jefferson's embargo policy with the greatest rapidity. The bill received the President's assent on December 22. Erskine sent the news to England on the next day with the comment that England's proclamation of October 17 convinced the Americans that Great Britain was determined to continue her impressment policy.

The American Embargo Act of December, 1807, concluded the first and contributed to the second phase of the origins of the War of 1812. The emphasis was now to change from seamen to ships and cargoes. In the Embargo Act, the gradual worsening of Anglo-American relations from 1804 to 1807, largely as a result of impressment, reached a culmination. After the *Chesapeake* incident of June, 1807, America had placed herself in a position in which, if England refused to meet the American demands, either war or some form of commercial retaliation was inevitable. Instead of obtaining a redress of her grievances, America was presented with the double blow of the statement from Canning that the *Chesapeake* incident could not be combined with a general agreement on impressments, and England's reassertion of her right of impressment in the October proclamation. When this was combined with the news of the enforcement of the Berlin Decree, and rumors of a stricter British commercial policy, it is not surprising that the reaction should have been in the form of economic sanctions rather than open warfare. The tradition of economic coercion was an old one in American history—even in the conflict resulting in the Revolution an attempt at economic coercion had long preceded actual warfare—and Jefferson and the men around him had frequently expressed their belief in the power of economic means to bring England to reason. This was the obvious occasion to give economic coercion a trial, and America, weak and uncertain of her power to wage war against the country that had defied Napoleon, attempted to defend her rights by peaceful rather than bellicose means. The reasons for the failure of this attempt are to be found in Europe, for even before America had resorted to her coercive device of the Embargo, the European war had at last developed into a vast commercial struggle between England and France. Now impressment was to take its place as only one of many American grievances. The origins of the War of 1812 were entering their second—their commercial—phase, and to understand this it is necessary to turn again to the internal politics of England.

3 FROM *Julius Pratt*
The Expansionists of 1812

The role of the West in bringing on the War of 1812 has long fascinated historians. That area of the United States provided vociferous leadership in Congress, for the war hawks were generally drawn from frontier constituencies. Furthermore, an examination of the final voting on the declaration shows that the West was nearly unanimous in giving its support to the President. Members from Kentucky, Tennessee, Vermont, and western Pennsylvania cast their votes for war. Although their votes were important, they were not critical, for the southern and middle states provided the bulk of the support for the President.

Nevertheless, the question remains as to why the frontier was so united in its view. Was it the consequence of land hunger? Certainly this was the view advanced by L. M. Hacker in "Western Land Hunger and the War of 1812," Miss. Valley Hist. Rev. X, 1924. Or was it due to a desire to end finally an Indian conspiracy supported by Britain in Canada? Professor J. W. Pratt searches for an answer to these intriguing questions in his Expansionists of 1812. He suggests that the West and the South had a joint interest in a war by which the one would gain Canada, and the other Florida. Professor Pratt does not dismiss the importance of maritime issues, but he does add another dimension to the explanation of the War of 1812.

THE WEST AND THE WAR OF 1812

That the United States went to war with Great Britain in 1812 at the insistence of western and southern men, and over the opposition of the Northeast, is a fact about which there has never been any doubt. There was a paradox here which apparently gave little concern to the older historians. If the real grievances which caused the war were interference by Great Britain with American commerce and the rights of American sailors, why was war to redress those grievances opposed by the maritime section of the nation and urged by the inland section, which they scarcely affected? The old answers, that New England was Anglophile, and that the West and South had developed a more aggressive and martial spirit, which felt the humiliation if not the pecuniary loss occasioned by the British

SOURCE. Julius Pratt, *The Expansionists of 1812*, pp. 9–15. Copyright 1925 by The Macmillan Company; renewed 1951 by Julius Pratt. Reprinted with permission of The Macmillan Company and the author.

measures, were in a measure true, but hardly sufficient. For some years past, historians have been turning to new explanations.

In this field, as in almost every other in American history, it is easy to see the profound influence of Professor F. J. Turner. Before the publication in 1893 of his essay, "The Significance of the Frontier in American History," the frontier had been regarded as little more than a picturesque phase in the national development. Since that event, the frontier—the "West"—has come to be recognized as the source of many aspects of American character and the determining factor in many American policies. It was natural, therefore, that students of the War of 1812 should come to view the West —particularly the Northwest—with more careful scrutiny. The result of such examination has been the placing of new emphasis upon the western demand for the annexation of Canada, which is seen to have arisen in large part from the conviction that the British were in league with the northwestern Indians and that only by destroying that alliance could the Northwest continue its career of expansion.

The war found its sponsors, however, not only in the Northwest but along the whole frontier from New Hampshire round about to Georgia. For the states south of Kentucky, there was little to be gained by the conquest of Canada, and, since the divergence of interests between North and South was already evident, there was reason for southern states to fear the political effect of a large addition to northern territory. Why, then, did the Southwest support the war? The answer to this question has been suggested, but has never been worked out with anything approaching completeness. The examination made in the course of this study reveals an ardent expansionist sentiment already at work along the whole southern and southwestern border, varying in scope from the relatively modest proposal for the annexation of the Floridas to the more visionary idea of seizing all the Spanish possessions on the continent of North America. The link between the designs of the Southwest and those of the Northwest was the existence of the alliance between Great Britain and Spain. It was widely assumed that war with Great Britain would mean war with Spain, and that thus expansion at the north and at the south would proceed *pari passu*.

The purposes of the present study have been: to examine the development in the Northwest of the demand for the conquest and annexation of Canada; to trace the rise in the South and Southwest of the plan to annex the Floridas and possibly Mexico; to discover

the relations of these two proposals to each other and to the
question of war with Great Britain; to determine the position of the
executive branch of the United States government (especially of
Madison and his Secretary of State, Monroe) toward the plans for
expansion, north and south; and finally, to determine the causes for
the failure, all along the line, of the expansionist hopes with which
the war began.

The principal conclusions arrived at may be summarized as
follows:

I. The belief that the United States would one day annex Canada
had a continuous existence from the early days of the War of Independence to the War of 1812. From 1783 to about 1810 such
annexation was thought of only as a matter for an indefinite future,
the nation during those years having neither the strength, nor any
sufficient motive, for taking Canada by force. The rise of Tecumseh,
backed, as was universally believed, by the British, produced an
urgent demand in the Northwest that the British be expelled from
Canada. This demand was a factor of primary importance in bringing on the war.

II. The South was almost unanimous in its demand for the
Floridas, for agrarian, commercial, and strategic reasons, and in the
spring of 1812 appeared to be in a fair way to accomplish its purpose. In the Southwest, at the same time, there was a lively interest
in Mexico and a widely prevalent opinion that it was ready to fall
into American hands.

III. Even within the Republican party, there was already a distinct
sectional rift between North and South, and neither section was
anxious to see the other increase its territory and population. But
if both could gain at the same time, and in something like equal
proportion, such objections would be obviated on both sides. There
is good evidence that, before the declaration of war, northern and
southern Republicans came to a definite understanding that the
acquisition of Canada on the north was to be balanced by the
annexation of the Floridas on the south. Thus the war began with a
double-barrelled scheme of territorial aggrandizement.

IV. Both Madison and Monroe, especially the latter as Secretary
of State, were wholly in sympathy with the proposal for annexing
Florida. The invasion of East Florida by General Mathews in March
and April, 1812, was effected with the full knowledge of the administration. Special circumstances forced the government to repudiate
Mathews, but the territory he had taken from the Spanish was held

for over a year, until Congress had twice refused to sanction the
occupation. At the same time, Monroe's official correspondence
shows that he never really desired or expected the annexation of
Canada.

V. It appears that in the all round failure of the expansionist
plans, sectional feeling played a larger part than is commonly supposed. The sectional bargain with which the war had begun broke
down. Opposition from northern Republicans combined with Federalists forced the abandonment of East Florida. On the other
hand, it is evident that in the utter failure of the efforts to take
Canada, not only want of skill and preparation, but also a lack of
enthusiasm on the part of the administration and of certain
southern men in Congress played a part.

VI. Finally, in the expansionist program with which the war
opened, we have the first general appearance of the idea which later
received the name of "Manifest Destiny." Although enthusiasts like
Jefferson had dreamed years before of a nation destined to embrace
the continent, the date usually given for the dawn of "Manifest
Destiny" is about 1830. Yet both in the Congressional debates of
1812 and in the contemporary press, particularly that of the Southwest, we find the idea repeatedly expressed. "Where is it written in
the book of fate," asked the editor of the Nashville Clarion (April 28,
1812), "that the American republic shall not stretch her limits from
the Capes of the Chesapeake to Nootka sound, from the isthmus of
Panama to Hudson bay?"

Two explanations are due, with respect to the scope and pro-
portions of this study. First, it makes no effort to give a full account
of the causes of the War of 1812, but deals with one set of causes
only. The exclusion from all but briefest mention of the maritime
grievances against Great Britain is with no wish to belittle them.
Without them, it is safe to say, there would have been no war, just
as the writer feels safe in saying that without the peculiar grievances and ambitions of the West there would have been no war. One
set of causes was perhaps as essential as the other.

Second, the writer has thought best to give some account of those
military operations during the war which bore a direct relation to
the plans for territorial expansion. The campaigns of 1812 and 1813
on the Canadian border are given in the barest outline, while the
operations in East Florida, though on a smaller scale, receive a more
detailed treatment. For this apparent lack of proportion the justification is that the details of the northern campaigns are well known

and can be read in a dozen careful accounts, whereas no full account
of the East Florida operations has ever been published.

4 FROM   *Bradford Perkins*
                 Prologue to War

*The economic disputes between Britain and the United States were clearly a major
cause of the War of 1812. Again, these disputes had their origin in the war in Europe.
France, having lost control of the high seas, attempted to impose a reverse blockade
on England through the Berlin and Milan decrees. These measures made liable for
seizure any neutral ship which, sailing for France, had either first called at a British
port or submitted to a search by the Royal Navy. Britain's measures were equally
punitive. She declared great stretches of the European coast blockaded, she insisted
that neutrals going to Europe should first call at a British port, and she enlarged the
definition of contraband so that it included foodstuffs as well as arms and accouterments
of war. The combination of these measures placed the United States in an intolerably
difficult position, since to obey the regulations of one would lead to the seizure of her
ships by the other. The weight of American criticism fell on Britain because she controlled the high seas and so could enforce her measures more rigorously and effectively.
It was Britain's refusal to modify her Orders in Council until it was too late that
played such an important part in bringing on the war. Professor Bradford Perkins
develops this argument fully in his* Prologue to War.

THE ORDERS IN COUNCIL AND THE WAR

Even more than impressment, with which congressmen and newspaper editors often coupled them, the Orders in Council showed
Britain's contemptuous disdain for American protests against her
use of sea power. The forcible enlistment of seamen could be expressed in dramatic human terms. The Orders in Council more
massively and more selfishly assaulted the United States. Their
material cost was impressive. Although the number of seizures
actually fell after 1808, the year beginning in October, 1811, saw an
increase of nearly 50 per cent. The orders and the *Essex* case had
long since reduced the reëxport trade to a shadow of its former size.

SOURCE. Bradford Perkins, *Prologue to War* (Berkeley and Los Angeles: University of
California Press, 1961), pp. 430–432. Reprinted by permission of the Regents of the
University of California and the author.

After a spurt stimulated by Macon's Bill No. 2 and the Cadore letter, the export of native American produce fell drastically after the spring of 1811. By far the greatest proportion of this decline came in exports to Britain, particularly because return cargoes were forbidden, and the United Kingdom suffered from glut. Agriculturists and plantation owners, some shipowners, and the average congressman ascribed the decline to Britain's Orders in Council, which prevented Americans from developing the presumably lucrative Continental market. At the same time, particularly because the British permitted their own subjects to trade with Europe under license, the Orders in Council seemed humiliating. Since at least November, 1807, the English had presumed to legislate not only for their own people but also for the commercial world. Economic necessity and national right alike cried out against the Orders in Council.

Everyone in Washington during the months from November to June placed the Orders in Council at the head of the list of American grievances. Louis Sérurier and Augustus Foster, Federalists and Republicans were in agreement. When the British minister asked Chauncey Goodrich, a Federalist senator, "what was required of us by Men of fair Views", he replied, "take off the Orders in Council and come to some Arrangement about Impressment." In November President Madison considered British maritime policy the transcendent issue between the two countries. Porter's report declared that the orders "went to the subversion of our national independence" and were "sapping the foundation of our prosperity." Throughout the winter congressmen assailed the orders, drowning out the "whip-poor-will cry" for Canada of which John Randolph spoke. Repeal, Madison noted years later, would have postponed war and led to renewed negotiations on impressment "with fresh vigor & hopes, under the auspices of success in the case of the orders in council." The orders, he told Jared Sparks in 1830, were the only issue sturdy enough to bear a declaration of war.

The strength of this issue depended in part upon the reinforcement provided by impressment and other grievances, the flying buttresses of the central structure. Had the orders stood alone as a British challenge, war would probably not have come in 1812. But they became the key to the drive for war. No other factor, not even impressment, which most directly affected Northeasterners, struck all sections so impartially. Not even impressment exceeded the orders as a threat to America's position as a sovereign power. The

Orders in Council were four years old when the Twelfth Congress met, going on five when America declared war. Why this delay? A natural desire to escape war partly explains it. Unreal faith in the power of trade boycotts, more justified expectations from the Erskine agreement, optimism engendered by the Cadore letter, hope that the Prince of Wales would replace his insane father's ministers with more friendly men, the anticipated impact of American measures of preparedness in Great Britain—all these counseled delay. When war ultimately came in June, 1812, the Orders in Council were the central issue. The requirements of consistency and a growing realization that American honor had been nearly exhausted were the immediate precipitants.

5 FROM   *Norman K. Risjord*
        1812 : Conservatives, War Hawks and the
                    Nation's Honor

The argument that it was land hunger or a desire to end British-backed Indian conspiracy which caused the War of 1812 has not proved wholly satisfying to some historians. The further suggestions that maritime issues or a depression in the Mississippi Valley attributable to the British Orders in Council tipped the scales have not convinced all students of the subject. A fresh perspective was offered by Professor Norman K. Risjord. He suggested that America was faced with the alternatives of submitting to British practices or fighting to preserve America's national honor. Clay, Calhoun, and others were deeply concerned over the affronts to America's pride and position. All the measures tried by previous administrations to put an end to these insults had failed and President Madison therefore felt that he had no choice but to issue a call to arms.

NATIONAL HONOR AND THE WAR

The modern tendency to seek materialistic motives and economic factors in all human relations has greatly obscured one of the basic causes of the War of 1812. A generation of historians, brought up on

SOURCE. Norman K. Risjord, "1812: Conservatives, War Hawks and the Nation's Honor," *William and Mary Quarterly*, Third Series, Vol. XVIII (April 1961), pp. 196–210. Reprinted by permission of the author.

the disillusionment that followed the failure of the attempt to "make the world safe for democracy" in 1919, has persistently searched for the hidden economic factors behind all wars. Yet a cursory glance at the statistics of American commerce in the first decade of the nineteenth century will show that the War of 1812 was the most uneconomic war the United States has ever fought. A casual search through the letters and speeches of contemporaries reveals that those who fought the war were primarily concerned with the honor and integrity of the nation.

Students of the period are familiar with the standard explanation for the war: the election of 1810, by providing 63 new faces in a House of 142, represented a popular disillusionment with the Jeffersonian system and supplied the new Twelfth Congress with a number of young war hawks, such as Henry Clay, John C. Calhoun, and Felix Grundy, who were determined to assert America's position in the world. Since the loudest demand for strong measures, as well as some of the ablest of the war hawks, came from the West, historians have been channeled into a search for reasons why the West should have demanded a war for "free trade and sailors' rights"; the historiography of the period has been almost exclusively concerned with "Western war aims." The desire for land, Canadian or Indian, fear of a British-backed Indian conspiracy, concern over the declining prices of agricultural products and the restriction of markets abroad—all at one time or another have been represented as basic causes of the war.

The weakness in this interpretation is that it virtually ignores the vote on the declaration of war in June 1812. The West may have been influenced by economic as well as patriotic motives, but the West, after all, had only ten votes in the House of Representatives. The South Atlantic states from Maryland to Georgia cast thirty-nine, or nearly half, of the seventy-nine votes for war in 1812. Any explanation of the war must place primary emphasis on the Southern Congressmen, and neither feature of the standard interpretation—the concept of a "revolution" in popular sentiment in 1810 and the emphasis on economic factors—satisfactorily explains their votes for war.

Most of these Southern Congressmen were "old Republicans," conservatives whose political Bible was the Republican platform of 1800 and who had sat in Congress for years. In the South there is no evidence of a sudden popular demand in the election of 1810 for a more energetic government and a more vigorous foreign policy. Maryland, which voted six to three for war in June 1812, had four new members in the Twelfth Congress, one a Federalist. The three new Republicans either won the election without opposition or they replaced men who had supported military preparations and a stronger foreign policy in the Eleventh Congress.

Virginia which held her elections for the Twelfth Congress in the spring of 1811, returned a virtually identical delegation of seventeen Republicans and five Federalists. The two Quids, John Randolph and Edwin Gray, were re-elected, as were most of the conservative Republicans of the Eleventh Congress. The Shenandoah Valley remained as solidly Federalist as it had been in 1800, and the tramontane region, the one part of the state that might have been concerned with Indians and Western lands, elected Thomas Wilson, its first Federalist since 1793.

Virginia's election as a whole produced five new Republican members; none apparently was elected on the issue of peace or war. John Wayles Eppes, the only strong leader Virginia had sent to the Eleventh Congress, moved to John Randolph's district in the Southside and was defeated by Randolph in the election. The contest was close even though Eppes never formally declared himself a candidate, but the objections to Randolph centered on his vigorous opposition to the Madison administration. No one maintained that the election of Eppes would ensure stronger measures toward Great Britain. Eppes's seat in his former district was taken by James Pleasants, a war Republican who in the postwar period was to revert to the old Jeffersonian strict constructionist doctrines. In Thomas Jefferson's own district, which included Albermarle County, David S. Garland was replaced by Hugh Nelson, a close friend of James Monroe and member of the "minority" that had supported Monroe against James Madison's election in 1808 because it felt that Madison was too nationalistic. Nelson entered the Twelfth Congress with a decided preference for peace at any price. In the Fredericksburg area the administration regular, Walter Jones, declined to run again, and in the election Major John P. Hungerford defeated John Taliaferro by six votes. Hungerford was a former Quid and had sat on the Monroe electoral committee in 1808. Taliaferro contested the election, received the support of the war hawks in the House, and was awarded the seat. In the Fauquier-Culpeper district John Love, who had generally supported preparedness measures in the Eleventh Congress, declined re-election and was replaced by another war Republican, Dr. Aylet Hawes.

Nearly half the Virginia Congressmen were elected without opposition, and even where there was a contest the election seldom turned on the issue of foreign policy. Typical of Virginia conservatives re-elected in 1811 was John Clopton, who had represented the Richmond district since 1801. If a letter to his constituents published in the *Virginia Argus* is a fair summary of his campaign platform, Clopton was running in support of the nonintercourse law and against the Bank of the United States, giving no indication of any departure from the Jeffersonian system. Clopton had two opponents, one of whom withdrew before the election, while the other made public statements agreeing with Clopton on every issue.

The election of 1810 in North Carolina similarly produced no great change in her representation. Of her twelve Congressmen eight were re-elected, two of them Federalists and one, Richard Stanford, a Randolph Quid. Two of the four newcomers had served in Congress during the Jefferson administration (William Blackledge from 1803 to 1808 and Thomas Blount from 1804 to 1808). The only new faces in the North Carolina group, Israel Pickens and William R. King, were war hawks, but neither defeated an incumbent.

The political "revolution" in South Carolina in the election of 1810, which produced a unanimous vote for war in June 1812, was more apparent than real. The election of the three great war hawk leaders, John C. Calhoun, William Lowndes, and Langdon Cheves, was more an addition of talent than of numbers to the war party in Congress. In the campaign Calhoun had openly advocated war, but he was elected without opposition since the incumbent—his cousin Joseph Calhoun, a war hawk in the Eleventh Congress—declined re-election and supported him. William Lowndes succeeded to the seat of John Taylor, one of the administration's floor leaders in the Eleventh Congress who had been elected to the Senate. Cheves was elected in 1810 to fill a vacant seat in the Eleventh Congress and was re-elected to the Twelfth.

The other prominent war hawk, David Rogerson Williams, took the seat of his brother-in-law Robert Witherspoon, who declined re-election and threw his support to Williams. Williams, moreover, as a member of the Ninth Congress, had followed John Randolph in rebellion against the Jefferson administration in 1806 and thus fits more into the pattern of the converted conservative. Indeed, as late as May 1812 a Federalist member of the House observed that Williams was still trying to make up his mind between peace and

war. The only real contest in South Carolina was the defeat of
Lemuel J. Alston by Elias Earle, but no current issue was involved
for the two men had taken turns defeating each other for years.

The election in South Carolina illustrates the real significance of
the election of 1810. Without any fundamental change in public
opinion, and partly by coincidence, South Carolina produced some
of the outstanding leaders of the Twelfth Congress. But the change,
as in the Western elections that produced Henry Clay and Felix
Grundy, was primarily in ability rather than in numbers. Indeed,
speaking strictly in terms of numbers, the actual war hawks elected
in 1810 were outvoted by Federalists and antiwar Republicans in the
Twelfth Congress. The young war hawks from the South and West
were certainly able men, and largely by force of character alone they
led an unwilling and apathetic country to war.

Yet was leadership alone enough? Several prominent war hawks
—Clay, Richard M. Johnson, Ezekiel Bacon, Cheves, and Peter B.
Porter—were members of the Eleventh Congress, but despite their
ability they had been unable to lead that body in any consistent
direction. At least as significant as the sudden appearance of a few
talented war hawks in the Twelfth Congress was the gradual conversion of the average Republican from Jeffersonian pacifism to a
vigorous defense of America's neutral rights. It was these men, most
of them Southerners who had been in Congress for years, who
provided the necessary votes for war, just as they had provided the
main support for the embargo and nonintercourse laws. Their
conversion seems to have stemmed primarily from a disillusionment
with the old system of commercial retaliation and a growing realization that the only alternative to war was submission and national
disgrace. Every expedient to avoid war honorably had been tried
without success. Submission to the orders in council presaged a
return to colonial status; war seemed the only alternative. The war,
at least as far as the South was concerned, was brought on by men
who had had a "bellyful" of England, not by men who were interested in Western lands, or Indians, or prices in the lower Mississippi Valley.

The major weakness in the various economic interpretations is
their failure to explain the demand for war in the Middle Atlantic
states and in the South. The "expansionist" school of historians,
with internal variations, generally maintains that the war was the
result of the Western desire for land, in Canada as well as in Indian-
dominated Indiana, and that the conquest of Canada was demanded

both for its own sake and because the British were backing the Tecumseh confederacy. The difficulty is that the areas most concerned with these problems—Indiana, Illinois, and Michigan— were territories with no vote in Congress. Even Ohio, which presumably had a direct interest in the Wabash lands, was by no means unanimously in favor of war. Its one representative, Jeremiah Morrow, voted for war in 1812 just as he had voted for the embargo in 1807, but Ohio's two senators, Thomas Worthington and Alexander Campbell, opposed war in 1812 because the nation was unprepared and they feared an Indian attack on the defenseless frontier. Both preferred to retain the old system of commercial retaliation. Some have suggested that Ohio's senators were out of touch with public sentiment, but a recent biographer of Worthington feels that a plebiscite held in the spring of 1812 would probably have shown a majority of the people of Ohio against war. Kentucky and Tennessee, it is true, showed considerable interest in the Indian lands and in Canada, but even so their votes in Congress were hardly enough to carry the country to war.

Julius W. Pratt, leading proponent of the "expansionist" thesis, circumvented this difficulty by conjecturing a "frontier crescent" of war hawks extending from New Hampshire (John A. Harper) to Kentucky (Clay and Johnson) and Tennessee (Felix Grundy) and ending in South Carolina (Calhoun, Lowndes, and Cheves) and Georgia (George M. Troup). Yet this seems an arbitrary conjunction of dissimilar areas. Why should New Hampshire or Vermont have been interested enough in the Wabash lands to go to war? And how explain a Southern interest in the Wabash or in Canada? Pratt plugged this hole by surmising a bargain between Southern and Western war hawks in which Florida would be brought into the Union to balance the conquest of Canada. The only evidence he cites, however, is one editorial in a Tennessee newspaper.

It is true that Southern war hawks talked much about the conquest of Canada, but they seem to have regarded it as primarily a method of conducting the war rather than as an ultimate objective. Secretary of State Monroe, for instance, felt that Canada might be invaded, "not as an object of the war but as a means to bring it to a satisfactory conclusion." On the other hand there is evidence that some Southerners actually feared the annexation of Canada. John Randolph certainly considered the possibility that Canada might be acquired the best of reasons for not going to war, and a fellow Virginian elected in 1810 wrote home in December 1811: "The

New Yorkers and Vermonters are very well inclined to have upper Canada united with them, by way of increasing their influence in the Union." As to the other half of the bargain there is little evidence that outside of the border area the South was much interested in Florida, and recent scholars have tended to minimize the importance of Florida in the Southern demand for war.

Somewhat more plausible is the economic interpretation of the war in terms of declining farm prices and the restriction of markets abroad. This point of view was first put forth in the early 1930's by George Rogers Taylor, who suggested that the declining price of agricultural products, particularly in the lower Mississippi Valley, may have been a factor in the Western demand for war. The gist of this argument is summed up in a letter of a Louisiana planter of July 25, 1811: "Upon the subject of cotton we are not such fools, but we know that . . . the British are giving us what they please for it. . . . But we happen to know that we should get a much greater price for it, for we have some idea of the extent of the Continent, and the demand there for it; . . . and, therefore, upon the score of lucre, as well as national honor, we are ready." More recently, this argument has been adopted to explain the West–South alliance. Both sections were concerned with the declining prices of the great staple exports, cotton, tobacco, and hemp, and were inclined to blame the British orders in council for restricting their markets. The South and West, in this view, went to war primarily to defend the right to export their products without interference from Britain.

That prices for these great staples declined gradually throughout the first decade of the century cannot be denied, but to what extent the British blockades were responsible is more difficult to determine. The direct trade in agricultural products was not generally affected by the orders in council; not till the winter of 1811–12 did the British interfere with cotton shipments, though their action at that time helped to justify war—at least in the mind of the North Carolina planter Nathaniel Macon. It is interesting, however, that despite the British orders the market for cotton was rapidly increasing both in quantity exported and in geographical area. The declining price was a long-term phenomenon only temporarily interrupted by the postwar prosperity, rather than a result of British restrictions. Statistics on the export of tobacco similarly give no real indication that the British orders in council were responsible for the constriction in markets or the drop in prices.

It is true, however, that the opinion that British restrictions were responsible for lower prices, even if unjustified, seems to have been widely held in the South. Margaret Kinard Latimer has recently brought to light evidence that this was a major factor in the demand for war at least in South Carolina. "Whether or not fighting a war with England," she concludes, "was the logical step to take as a remedy to the commercial and thus agricultural distress is not the question—the South Carolinians of 1812 were convinced that a war would help." Yet this leaves unanswered the question of why South Carolinians preferred to ignore the probability that war would further disrupt their commerce, while others, notably the New Englanders, were so painfully aware of it. Is it possible that those South Carolina politicians who stressed the cotton depression as a cause for war were merely supplying additional reasons that might influence the wavering?

It must also be remembered that the decline in prices was not universal. Prices for beef, corn, and flour, the main exports of the Middle Atlantic states, actually increased over the decade, while the price of pork declined only slightly. In 1810–11 total exports in these products nearly doubled as American farms fed the Duke of Wellington's army in Spain. Pennsylvania, which voted sixteen to two for war with England, can hardly have been following the dictates of economic interest.

The South and the Middle Atlantic states, whose Congressmen furnished the major support for war, had little to gain economically from the conflict. Their direct trade in agricultural products was scarcely affected by the orders in council, and England had long been the major foreign market for both sections. Indeed, it might even be argued that these sections stood to lose as much by war as did New England. When, therefore, Nathaniel Macon spoke of going to war "to obtain the privilege of carrying the produce of our lands to a market"—an oft-quoted passage—he undoubtedly had in mind the "privilege" as much as the trade. Southerners went to war primarily to defend their rights, not their purses.

This is not to deny that economic factors were present. The final synthesis of the causes of the war will have to take into account various material factors—the fear of an Indian conspiracy in the West, for instance, and the concern over declining prices in the South—but it will also have to recognize that none of these economic theses furnishes a satisfactory explanation for the general demand for war. The only unifying factor, present in all sections of the country, was the growing feeling of patriotism, the realization that something must be done to vindicate the national honor. In recent years historians have tended more and more to stress this factor, particularly in its influence on the West, where a feeling of national pride was an obvious concomitant of the youth and exuberance of that section. Even Julius W. Pratt admitted that the war fever in the West "was doubtless due to various causes—perhaps most of all to sheer exasperation at the long continued dilatory fashion of handling the nation's foreign affairs." This factor was probably even more important in the Middle Atlantic states and in the South where fewer material interests were at stake.

The system of commercial retaliation itself had not been defended on economic grounds. The first nonintercourse resolution had been introduced in the spring of 1806 by a Pennsylvanian, Andrew Gregg, as an instrument for gaining by peaceful means some recognition of America's neutral rights. The embargo and the later nonintercourse laws were intended to furnish the President with a lever of negotiation, to maintain the national dignity short of war; it was the growing disillusionment with this system, the growing feeling that war was the only means for maintaining the nation's integrity that eventually brought on the conflict. This mental conversion is aptly illustrated by the following letter of John Clopton of Virginia:

"Let us consider what our government has done—how long it has borne with the repeated injuries which have been touched on in this letter—how often negotiations have been resorted to for the purpose of avoiding war; and the aggressions, instead of having been in any measure relaxed have been pursued with aggravating violence without a single ray of expectation that there exists any sort of disposition in the B[ritish] Cabinet to relax, but the strongest disposition to persist in their career.

". . . The outrages in impressing American seamen exceed all manner of description. Indeed the whole system of aggression now is such that the real question between G. Britain and the U. States has ceased to be a question merely relating to certain rights of commerce about which speculative politicians might differ in opinion—it is now clearly, positively, and directly *a question of independence,* that is to say, whether the U. States are really an independent nation."

Not all Republicans came to a similar conclusion at the same time. The process was a gradual one, beginning with the *Chesapeake* affair and the failure of the embargo to secure a recognition of American rights. The prominent Virginia Republican, Wilson Cary Nicholas, was one of the first to conclude that war was inevitable. Shortly after the Randolph schism in 1806, Nicholas had entered Congress at the behest of Jefferson, who needed an able floor leader in the House. The failure of the embargo convinced him that the whole policy of commercial retaliation was unsound, for it could not be enforced effectively enough to coerce the belligerents and it resulted only in the ruin of American agriculture. Since the Madison administration was unwilling to abandon the policy, Nicholas, rather than go into opposition, resigned his seat in the autumn of 1809. "We have tried negotiation until it is disgraceful to think of renewing it," he wrote Jefferson. "Commercial restrictions have been so managed as to operate only to our own injury. War then or submission only remain. In deciding between them I cannot hesitate a moment." George Washington Campbell of Tennessee reached a similar conclusion shortly after the *Chesapeake* affair, and he became one of the leading advocates for military preparations in the Tenth and Eleventh Congresses.

The gradual realization of the need for a more militant foreign policy was also reflected in the prominent Republican newspapers. Thomas Ritchie of the Richmond *Enquirer* considered the embargo the only honorable alternative to war, and when it was repealed Ritchie and the *Enquirer* began openly advocating war with England. William Duane, editor of the Philadelphia *Aurora,* generally supported the system of commercial retaliation, but the repudiation of David Erskine's agreement and the mission of Francis "Copenhagen" Jackson in the fall of 1809 convinced him that Britain did not intend to negotiate the question of neutral rights. By December 1809 he was advocating military preparations, the arming of American merchant ships, and, if those measures failed to intimidate Britain, "defensive war".

The old Jeffersonian, Nathaniel Macon, struggled long and valiantly with his conscience in an effort to reconcile Republican dogma with the obvious need for a vigorous defense of American rights. Throughout the Eleventh Congress he had been one of the administration leaders in the House, yet his basic conservatism was frequently evident. In the spring of 1810 he co-operated with John Randolph's efforts to reduce the size of the army and navy, even advocating that they be abolished altogether. As chairman of the foreign relations committee, Macon reported the nonintercourse

bill of April 1810, known as Macon's Bill Number Two, but he
personally opposed it because he felt it too provocative. Not until
the beginning of the Twelfth Congress did he reach the conclusion
that war was the only alternative. War was justified, he told the
House in December 1811, because of the recent British seizures of
ships carrying American agriculture products. This new aggression,
he felt, showed that the British, instead of becoming more lenient,
were actually tightening their system, and that further negotiation
was useless. Macon thereafter co-operated with the war hawks but
with some reluctance and with an occasional lapse. He voted against
every effort to increase the size of the navy, and he consistently
opposed all efforts during the session to raise the taxes to finance
the war.

A number of Republicans, though they co-operated with the
preparedness measures of the war hawks, could not make up their
minds on the basic issue of peace or war until the last minute. As
late as May 1812 a Massachusetts Federalist reported, perhaps
somewhat wishfully, that a majority of the Virginia delegation was
still against war. Besides the Federalists and the Quids, Randolph
and Gray, he listed Taliaferro, Nelson, William A. Burwell, John
Smith, and Matthew Clay as opposed to war. Representative of
this group was Hugh Nelson. Nelson had been elected in 1811, but
entered the Twelfth Congress with a lingering sympathy for the
old Republican "minority" whose leader was John Randolph of
Roanoke and whose prophet was John Taylor of Caroline. "I am a
messmate of J[ohn] R[andolph]," he wrote to a friend in Charlottesville shortly after his arrival in Washington. "The more I see him
the more I like him. He is as honest as the sun, with all his foibles,
and as much traduced I believe as any man has ever been. . . . Do
not be surprised if before the session closes I am classified with him
as a minority man." Nelson's maiden speech in the House came on
the resolution to increase the size of the regular army. It was a
rehash of all the old Republican antiwar arguments—war would
centralize the government, strengthen the executive, burden the
people with taxes, armies, and navies, undermine our "republican
simplicity," and subvert the Constitution. "I care not for the prices
of cotton and tobacco as compared with the Constitution," he
averred. Moreover he felt it unlikely that the United States could
ever gain recognition of her neutral rights, particularly since the
only program the war hawks suggested was a territorial war begun
by an invasion of Canada. Canada could not be conquered, but even

if it could, would this enforce our rights ? "Certainly not. The way to enforce these rights was by way of a great maritime force, which the nation were incompetent to raise and support." Nelson nevertheless felt the country should prepare for any eventuality because unless Britain relented there was no alternative to war. "I shall vote for the increase of the regular force," he concluded, "to go hand in hand with my friends, even in a war, if necessary and just." The most important of these friends was Nelson's neighbor from Charlottesville, Secretary of State Monroe, who by the spring of 1812 was a vigorous advocate of strong measures. In June, John Randolph wrote to John Taylor of Caroline that Monroe was "most furiously warlike & carries the real strength of the Southern representation with him."

Even more important than the personal influence of Monroe was the stimulus provided by President Madison. Most of the conservatives considered themselves loyal Republicans and were accustomed to following Presidential leadership in dealing with Britain and France. The policy of commercial retaliation had been largely an administration measure, and when the Twelfth Congress assembled in November 1811 Congress naturally looked to the Executive for guidance. Madison not only encouraged the war fever but he cooperated with the war hawks to a degree that has only recently begun to be fully recognized. His Annual Message to Congress in November 1811 outlined a program of military and naval preparations that was adopted virtually intact by the war hawks. His release of the correspondence of Captain John Henry in March 1812 and his request in April for a thirty-day embargo as a prelude to war have been interpreted by his most recent biographer, Irving Brant, as attempts to stimulate the war sentiment in Congress.

The war hawks took full advantage of these moves by the President in their efforts to hold the conservatives in line. In the later stages of the session, when a number of Republicans began to get cold feet, the war hawks informed them that it was too late to back out. When in April the bill initiating a temporary embargo was reported for debate, Henry Clay warned the House that if it stopped now after all the war measures it had passed, it would cover itself "with shame and indelible disgrace." That this argument was effective is indicated by John Smilie, who followed Clay on the floor. Smilie, whose western-Pennsylvania Republicanism dated back to the fight over the Constitution in 1787, admitted that from the beginning of the session he had only reluctantly voted for the various proposals of the war hawks. He actually preferred continuing commercial retaliation to a war and an army of 25,000. But he realized it was too late to back down now; the nation's honor was at stake: "If we now recede we shall be a reproach to all nations."

Added to this internal stimulus was the pressure of continuing British intransigence. On May 22 dispatches arrived in Washington from British Foreign Secretary Lord Castlereagh that contained nothing but a restatement of the British position. President Madison himself concluded that this was the last formal notice intended by the British government and sent his war message to Congress on June 1. It is not difficult to conceive that many a reluctant Republican came to the same decision.

It was thus with mixed motives that a majority of Republicans followed the war hawks to war. It is nevertheless clear that a primary factor in the mind of each was the conclusion that the only alternative to war was submission to the British commercial system. The balance of power in the House was held by men who had been in Congress for years, who had tried every expedient short of war to secure a recognition of American rights, and who at last had become surfeited with British commercial regulations. The war hawks, it is true, provided with their skill and energy the necessary impetus to war, but they could not have done so had not a majority of the Republican Party, particularly in the South, become gradually converted to the idea that war was the only alternative to national humiliation and disgrace. In this sense the war hawks acted as the intangible catalyst for a reaction whose basic elements were already present.

Roger Brown
The Republic in Peril: 1812

The United States entered the War of 1812 with its Congress divided and its
people uncertain. The debate in Congress over the President's war message was
long and closely argued. There were some who still called for delay, saying that
America was not yet ready for military combat. There were others who demanded
war with France as well as Britain, although no one knew how one could fight such a
triangular conflict. There were even some who continued to argue that Britain should
not be engaged for she remained the last hope of ordered government in a world
shattered by revolutionary war.

But a majority wanted war and got it. Who made up that majority? And who
constituted the minority? On what grounds did people oppose the President? Why
did two states as similar in population and structure as Pennsylvania and New York
elect members who voted in an almost diametrically opposite fashion? And why did
the southern and middle states support the war while New England generally opposed
it? Professor Roger Brown addresses himself to these questions and provides answers
to them in his Republic in Peril: 1812.

PARTY POLITICS AND THE WAR

Integrity, intelligence, and devotion to public interest—these were
the personal attributes needed for able, responsible leadership at
home and abroad. There was no room for these qualities in the
Federalist view of their opponents. How could an administration
devoted principally to perpetuating its own power deal competently
with pressing national problems? One could pretty well predict
Federalist reaction when Republicans undertook to protect American commerce during the wars of Napoleon.

When British seizure of American merchantmen began after the
Essex decision in 1805 the Federalists castigated their Republican
opponents for failure to protect American shipping. It was an easy
matter to put the blame on Republican demagoguery, incompetence, and weakness. Presumably to court popularity at home, the
administration had slashed military, naval, and defense establish-

SOURCE. Roger Brown, *The Republic In Peril: 1812* (New York: Columbia University
Press, 1964), pp. 161–176. Reprinted by permission of the publisher.

ments, and had repealed all taxes, but had never given a thought to the invitation thus held out to foreign nations to plunder our commerce. Not even the most anglophile Federalist would deny that British seizures could not be permitted to continue. But to bring seizures to an end, a special mission composed of men of ability and character—who else but Federalists?—should be named to negotiate with Great Britain. Certainly the current American negotiator, James Monroe, a despicable pro-French Virginia politician, was neither qualified nor competent to carry out such a task.

The Federalists characteristically opposed nonimportation, the embargo, and subsequent restrictive measures. The fact that these were measures of despised and suspected party adversaries does more to explain the instantaneous and united opposition of Federalism than do all the theories hypothesizing Federalists as the champions of commerce or of Britain's fight against Napoleon. Thus Federalists looked upon the Republican nonimportation proposals of 1806 as chiefly designed to court popularity in a country angry at British aggressions. The disadvantages in such legislation were easy to find—once one set out to look for them. Federalists soon built up the case that commercial restrictions were irritating and provocative, obstacles rather than inducements to settlement. They argued that restrictions hurt American commercial interests far more than British interests. Their reaction to the embargo was even more extreme. They considered the measure deliberately framed to destroy commerce in order ultimately to desolate the northeast and perpetuate southern dominance of the nation. They even believed that Napoleon himself was behind the new policy. Either the French dictator had bullied or cajoled the American President into support of his anti-British Continental System. Everyone knew, of course, that Jefferson manipulated American anglophobia to suit his own political ambition. Until now few suspected him of such weakness as to permit a foreign potentate to dictate American foreign policy. No wonder men were gloomy at the prospect of continued Republican rule, and could write as did one Federalist: "The sky is lowering. What it will produce no one can tell. That the Administration is bent on checking the spirit of Commerce, and gradually undermining it I have no doubt. That it is favorably disposed towards the French Government I more than Suspect." Federalists ignored all arguments in behalf of the preventive and coercive functions of the embargo, but seized on its presumed foreign origin, its destructive effect on commerce, its corrupting influence on public morality, and its probable impeding effect on negotiation.

The Republicans argued that Great Britain was to blame for the continued controversy over neutral rights. Federalists took the contrary position that nothing stood in the way of friendly relations with Great Britain except Republican hostility, aggressiveness, and refusal to settle outstanding issues. Was not Jefferson's demand for an end to impressment made in the knowledge that Britain, who needed sailors to man her wooden walls against Napoleon, could not agree? Were not our periodic warnings and preparations for war deliberately made to gall her? Were not restrictive measures irritating to her statesmen? A Federalist congressman from Connecticut, James Hillhouse, spoke for many when he said that he believed it possible to resolve issues between the two nations "provided our Government are sincere in their wishes to preserve peace, and a good understanding with that nation. [Of] that I have my doubts, judging from the irritating measures adopted, and the unfriendly disposition manifested on every occasion which offers." Federalists came to believe settlement attainable only through repeal of all commercial restrictions, a strengthening of military and naval forces, and friendly, firm, able negotiation. A prominent Federalist senator from Connecticut, Chauncey Goodrich, affirmed in 1810: "Our course is to use endeavours to free our commerce from the fangs of the Law, to fortify our most prominant harbours, to equip and man our navy—to provide means of defence—and there to pause." He was confident, as he made clear on another occasion, that we could then adjust all points at issue—"I mean," he qualified, "if the negociation was ably conducted [!]" This, of course, was a plan that administration Republicans regarded as submission.

As the controversy continued, Federalists begun to feel confident that Jefferson and his party were playing an evil and sinister game with the international situation. These Republicans had no intention of coming to terms with Great Britain at all. They intended to keep relations with her in a state of exacerbation. Confidence became obsession as more evidences accumulated. Repeated warnings of war seemed calculated to anger British public opinion and prevent concessions to the United States. The nonintercourse law, opening commerce with all nations except the two European belligerents, bolstered Republican popularity by easing the hardships of the embargo, but at the same time it kept up the quarrel. Madison's interpretation of the ambiguous Cadore letter, which led to resumption of the nonimportation act, was an open revelation of his desire to avoid an accommodation.

Then did the Republican leaders want war? Federalists did not think so. War, with all its hardships and sacrifices, was bound to prove unpopular, and would end in disgrace under such incompetent leadership. On the other hand, a state of continued controversy enabled the Republicans to pose as defenders of American rights and honor against British aggression. This would win them popularity among the unthinking anti-British masses. At the same time, they could placate Napoleon by supporting his Continental System with commercial restrictions. Chauncey Goodrich stated the view of many colleagues when he wrote:

"Our administration will not treat with England;—that would offend Bonaparte & their friends; they will not fight, because that will shake them from their seats. The present irritable state of things answers the purposes of party at home, & keeps up the public passions to such a point as follows after the Administration in their restrictions on British commerce."

Another New England Federalist, Timothy Pickering, reemphasized this opinion:

"Mr Jefferson & Mr Madison, amidst numberless fair professions, have never seriously intended an adjustment of our differences with G. B. While they have ascribed the failure of all their negotiations to her injustice and inadmissible claims Villifying, at the same time, the whole body of the federalists, as the friends of G. B., as under her influence, and willing to sacrifice our just rights to her unwarrantable pretensions.

"Thus viewing their French connection to be essential to their existence as the dominant party; & fearing also the power of Bonaparte, at whose feet ere this time Mr. Jefferson confidently pronounced that proud Britain was to have fallen—the administration have not dared to come to any settlement with her on any one point: for the adjustment of that single point would remove one cause of popular irritation, and loosen one cord by which they hold the people. By such management they hope to preserve their power, avoiding a war with G. B. so long as Bonaparte will be contented with a *neutrality* so *hostile* towards that nation."

Even Madison's brief agreement with the British minister, David Erskine, made in April, 1809, and repudiated by Foreign Secretary

Canning two months later, could fit this view. The Federalists would not consider the agreement to be evidence of administration willingness to terminate disputes, but deemed it a consequence of their own efforts to force the administration to settle. As the Federalist Rufus King wrote: "One side rejoice because they think that the Embargo &c. has brought England to terms, and the other side rejoice because they believe that the opposition to the late Measures of Congress has obliged the administration to abandon their system, and to accept a Reconciliation with England."

The 12th Congress that voted war included 43 Federalist members. Of the 40 Federalist congressmen and senators actually voting, all cast votes against war. Nor do the figures sustain a sectional interpretation of this vote. True, 31 Federalists against war came from northern constituencies. But it is seldom noted that 9 Federalists who voted against war came from south of the Mason–Dixon line. Twenty-three percent of the Federalist vote against war came from southern members of the party. Outside Congress Federalists condemned the measure. Federalist newspapers denounced it. Federalist-controlled town meetings and state legislatures passed condemnatory resolutions. Federalist merchants and shopkeepers closed places of business when they heard the news, Federalist deacons tolled church bells, and Federalist ship captains lowered their colors to half-mast. Everywhere, north and south, Federalism stood against the war. Was this typical Federalist negativism to all things Republican? The private letters of congressional Federalists reveal that it was so.

Republican senators and congressmen voted for war because they believed there was no other acceptable alternative. President Madison had taken the position that everything possible short of war had been tried and failed. Britain would persist in her Orders in Council until forced to retract by measures of force. Republicans believed the President and voted for war when the time came to do so.

No Federalist would accept these views. The very idea that the administration had tried everything in its power was absurd. How could anyone accept this argument when everyone knew that the Republican leaders had done their utmost to avoid settlement with Great Britain? Unneutral and unfriendly commercial restrictions, rejection of the Monroe–Pinkney treaty, threats and menaces of war, unfair and extreme demands—all these heightened the controversy, as Republicans intended they should do. Most Federalists agreed

with Republicans in condemning the Orders in Council as un-
acceptable infringements on American commerce and sovereignty.
This certainly did not mean that the time had finally come to go to
war. There had yet to take place a sincere and unprejudiced effort
to obtain repeal of the Orders. "Certain it is," wrote Samuel
Taggart of Massachusetts, "that no fair attempt has been made on
the principles of candid negotiation to obtain a redress of our
wrongs; especially since our disputes began to assume a serious
aspect in the years 1805, 6." The Republicans have sought consistently to frighten Great Britain into concessions, to extort them
from her fears. The nonimportation act of 1806, the embargo, the
nonintercourse law, the late nonimportation policy, and the present
threat of war "are all of this complexion and all have been equally
abortive and probably have been so intended by the American
government." Therefore, repeal all commercial restrictions and
appeal to that power in a firm and friendly manner to do us justice.

Neither would Federalists believe that Republicans seriously
meant war. No one with any knowledge of Republicans and their
past behavior could doubt that war was anything but bluff. All the
war talk and military preparations were a cheap political trick to
court popularity and discredit the Federalist party. A war declared
by these cynical demagogues would prove politically disastrous, as
they well knew, for with no good cause for war, the people would
soon tire of sacrifice and topple those responsible from power.
But by threatening war the Republicans, in the forthcoming spring
and fall elections, could exploit expected Federalist opposition.
When the American public saw Federalists oppose Republican
military measures they would identify the Federalists with "Toryism"
and vote for the party that stood up manfully to a life-long enemy.
Meanwhile the Republicans would have backed out of the war and
returned to commercial restrictions, anticipating Federalist relief
from escape from war and acquiescence in continuation of peace. . . .

More familiar to students of this period was the Federalist
hypothesis that pitted Republican "war hawks" against "peace
men" in an intraparty struggle over future policy. A conflict of this
kind seemed plausible enough. Belligerent speeches from freshman
Republican congressmen contrasted sharply with vague warnings
from the President and members seeking to leave Great Britain a
path of escape. The presumed struggle was at its peak when Quincy
informed Oliver Wolcott, Jr., in April that the Executive had
utterly failed to prepare the country for war but congressmen were

insisting that "'war must & will be declared'—now—before the end of ninety days." The scene seemed "absolutely incomprehensible" except on the "hypothesis that administration have no policy, except Embargo—that there is in the house of Representatives a strong party for war—that they counteract each other, and that the result is wholly problematical."

Taking note of the western origin of belligerent-sounding congressmen, Samuel Taggart found war party motivation explainable in terms of sectional politics. War men from the west knew that war "would bring distress and ruin incalculable upon the maritime frontier," thus forcing eastern inhabitants to seek safety in the interior and enriching and populating western states. Catching at Republican discussion regarding the conquest and possible annexation of Canada, other Federalists attributed "war hawk" policy to imperialist ambitions. "These backwoods-men mean that a predatory invasion of Canada shall avenge our commercial rights," avowed Quincy. Elijah Brigham charged that we are engaged in "a war of invasion to get possession of the Canadas on the north . . . a war of Ambition a war of conquest—having no other specific object but the conquest of the Canadas," a war of "rapine & plunder." Building on statements and legislation connecting Canada with Florida for invasion purposes, Federalists even presumed a bargain between northern and southern expansionists to annex both territories. The Federalist senator from Rhode Island, William Hunter, in 1813 publicly made such a charge:

"Last year the propositions to seize East Florida and to conquer Canada were associated. The inducements then held out were, an enlargement and arrondissement of the territory at the two extremeties; a fair division of the spoil. We consent that you may conquer Canada, permit us to conquer Florida. The declaration that Canada should be conquered and retained was the exacted pledge of the Northern men who voted for war."

What of the Republicans who did not want war, notably President Madison and his immediate supporters? The answer was plain: the "war hawks" had blackmailed them into support of their plan. In memoirs written long after the war was over, Josiah Quincy recalled the incident as well as if it had happened the day before. President Madison "was heart and soul a convert to Jefferson's policy, and held to the commercial restrictive system with the grasp of death." A war, he thought, would put an end to chances of re-

election. Nor did he "quit this grasp till waited upon by a committee of which Henry Clay was the Chairman, and was plainly told
that his being supported as the party candidate for the next Presidency depended upon his screwing his courage to a declaration of
war." Reluctantly, the Virginian had acceded, made a formal war
recommendation to Congress, and won a second term. "On this
combination of violence with individual interest and ambition was
laid the foundation of the war of 1812 with Great Britain." . . .

Republican assertions to the contrary, Federalists condemned this
war as utterly unjustified. No Federalist ever accepted the Republican argument that no other course remained. How could anyone
do so when the most promising solution of all had not yet been
tried? And when, as everybody knew, the Republican administration
had deliberately avoided settlement since Great Britain first began
her depredations? Spurning Republican contrary assertions, the
Federalists conjured up various alternative hypotheses, all presum-
ing corrupt and unconscionable motives. Not that these Federalist
myths lacked semblances of truth. Republicans, as we have seen, did
feel as the session wore on that party honor demanded war. Republicans did discuss Canada and Florida as the twin targets of
offensive operations, they did talk about annexing Canada, and they
did couple measures to establish temporary government and assure
protection to inhabitants in both these areas. Clay did visit the
President—but not to threaten him.

Some Federalists were not altogether content with these explanations, but looked for other motives. In September, 1812, Benjamin
Stoddert of Maryland, formerly secretary of the navy in John
Adams's cabinet, sought the views of a prominent North Carolina
Federalist on the matter. "Do you not see clearly, that not one of
the pretences for War, was the real cause[?]" he asked. "Where is
the real cause to be found? I wish I could answer with proofs, that
question." Just one day later Stoddert wrote to another Federalist,
in whose discretion he felt more confidence, that Napoleonic
pressure was the cause of war. Federalists who believed that Republican "war hawks" had dragooned the President were wrong,
he declared. All evidence that Madison and his advisers had opposed
the war had actually been "contrived with a view to make it," and
"Congress were made to act the part they did, during the last
session, by his & Gallatin's, and Jefferson's contrivances." This
remarkable feat of legislative prestidigitation had been performed
on orders from the French Emperor. Either Napoleon had bribed

these men to carry out his plans, or had blackmailed them. "The war, I have no doubt, is in subserviency to the views of France. Whether these men are actually sold to France—or whether Bonaparte has secrets of theirs which must not be disclosed, if the ruin of this Country will prevent it, I cannot determine—But this War, is entirely for French objects."

Did Federalists fear the consequences from such a war as this? Almost unanimously historians attribute Federalist opposition to concern for the safety of commerce and shipping. On the contrary, many Federalists predicted ultimate benefits to themselves and the country from this war. Its corrupt basis, the heavy American losses in goods and produce at home and abroad, the unprepared state of the nation, and the Republican incompetence in managing the war —all these circumstances would surely bring eventual political disaster to their opponents. There might be lives lost, shipping destroyed, and commerce disrupted; the British navy might bombard a seaport or two. But these were of less consequence than the benefit war would bring. At long last America would awaken to the real nature of present leadership and return the Federalists to power.

Thus Josiah Quincy, Jr., urged colleagues to "look definitely, to the fact of a possibly resulting war and analise its fair consequences and see, whether in truth, much of the evils are not those of imagination; and whether the fact of such a war would not crush the political influence of those, who should induce it." Abijah Bigelow of Massachusetts, foreseeing that war might be "the means of putting down an administration unfit, both in talents and integrity," remarked when war was declared that if the people failed to entrust national leadership "to more able hands our case is rather desperate, but I trust a proper remedy will be applied, before it is too late." A notable letter from Governor Roger Griswold of Connecticut carried the firm assurance of the benefit war would bring. "But if the event really happens, I make no doubt that it will produce a better state of things than the present." Outerbridge Horsey showed little fear of the impending decision: "Never did I till now so much rejoice that the people are sovereign, They must speak—and no doubt will speak with the celerity of lightening & the voice of thunder." Even James Bayard doubted that Britain would seek to make the war "active and destructive" against the country, and "probably a change of sentiment among the People may render it a war of no great duration." Indeed, Benjamin Tallmadge of Connecticut reported that "many" Federalists thought war would

drive the Republicans from power. A Federalist sympathizer visiting
Washington in June reported that the "federalists think this measure
likely to produce an ultimate benefit to the country; as it will, in all
probability, be the means of pulling down the present unprincipled
administration." Small wonder that Federalists could report "high
spirits" and "a good degree of composure" among colleagues on
the eve of war.

Did any Federalists hold a contrary view, that there were more
adversities than benefits in war? Some, a minority, did look upon
war with genuine fear of the consequences. Tallmadge of Connecticut did not anticipate the revolution in public sentiment so strongly
counted on by colleagues. Such a complete reversal seemed unlikely—he was "not so sanguine as many, who fully believe that such
an Event would change the whole political face of our Country."
His mood when war began was one of unrelieved gloom and fore-
boding. With Republican defeat at the polls unlikely, there was
reason to fear much from the continued leadership of such unprincipled and irresponsible men—most of all, an independence-
ending alliance with the European tyrant, Bonaparte: "Heaven only
knows what our Destiny is to be; but my fears forebode every Evil—
As the Cap to the Climax, I dread that above all, which Shall link
us to the fortunes, & chain us to the Carr of the French Emperor."
Joseph Pearson of North Carolina feared ultimate disaster. Announcing the commencement of hostilities to a party colleague, he
forecast an eventual French alliance. "France is our loving friend &
will no doubt soon be our ally— In what those dreadful measures
will end—God only knows—If the people do not interpose their
constitutional power—I fear all is lost." And Leonard White of
Massachusetts, three days after passage of the war bill, voiced dread
of "the current which is hurrying us to destruction. The situation in
which the Country is now placed causes the mind to shudder at the
thought of." Great Britain has the power to bring destruction to
our defenseless coastal cities and towns and capture our vessels in
her ports and on the ocean. She can seize American property of
great value in her warehouses. Lacking credit to borrow or funds to
carry on war without resort to taxes, driven to the ruinous expedient
of paper money, having neither a navy to protect our coasts nor an
army to defend our northern and western frontiers—"in this
deplorable situation we are plunged into a war with a nation who
has in her power to do us every injury, & all to gratify the malice &
revenge of a few men who see & know the people are not with

them." But "what is more than all to be dreaded & feared is an alliance with the Emperor of France which must naturally & most assuredly will be the consequence of this measure, unless the people rise in the majesty of their strength & at the approaching elections put it out of the power of those now in office to consummate the total wretchedness & misery of the Country."

Thus, when Federalists voted against the Republican war they did so out of a curious mixture of motives. On the one hand, while some gloomily prophesied disastrous consequences, others anticipated great political advantages from this war. They believed the temporary evils of war a price well worth paying when it meant defeat of political adversaries and restoral of the country to responsible, able, and high-minded Federalist leadership. But to reap the benefits war would bring, Federalists must of course go on record as opposed to the conflict. On the other hand, all believed war to be avoidable, unnecessary, and founded in unconscionable motives. The integrity of this moral disapproval is revealed in private correspondence. Pearson of North Carolina denounced the war to a party colleague as "Democratic folly & wikedness." Quincy castigated war as "unnecessary and wicked," and vowed that administration men "cannot justify the principle of such [a] war." William Reed of Massachusetts called war "an Act, I could not vote for, believing it inexpedient & wicked." Brigham referred to it as "this wicked and foolish war." Chittenden termed it a decision for which Republicans were "unable to give satisfactory reasons, why or wherefore." Though divided among themselves as to the relative benefits and evils in war, Federalists were united in a common spirit of genuine moral disapproval.

7 FROM   *Patrick C. T. White*
A Nation on Trial: America and the War of 1812

The current debate over Viet Nam in the United States reveals the deep doubts and passionate concern over the wisdom of America involving herself in a land war in Asia. In 1812 the same lack of consensus on national policy existed. It was quite clear by that year, however, that the President and a majority of his countrymen had decided that the country had reached the point where further submission to British practices would pose a greater threat to the nation's stability and future than going to war. Some still argued that a war would imperil the Republic. But even more insisted that a failure to fight would jeopardize the future of republicanism itself. It was not just America's interests, but rather her sovereignty that was being challenged. For a newly independent nation, such a challenge could not be ignored. This view is elaborated by Professor Patrick C. T. White in A Nation on Trial.

AMERICAN SOVEREIGNTY AND THE WAR

This was not a war entered upon with national fervor or romantic enthusiasm. There were, of course, some who felt that the battles would be short and victory swift. Canada, with its large American population, would fall to the famous Kentucky militia in a week. Jefferson wrote that "the acquisition of Canada this year, as far as the neighborhood of Quebec, will be a mere matter of marching. . . ." Events were to prove how foolish such a conception was. The war would be long and bloody—and many of the engagements fierce and closely fought. Those who envisaged an arduous and prolonged adventure were right—they almost always are. But apart from a few enthusiasts, America entered the conflict in a troubled state of mind. And for a century and a half various theories have been offered in explanation of this reluctance.

In 1939 there was a clear consensus in Britain that Hitler should be opposed, and in that fateful September when Poland was invaded, hardly a voice was raised against a declaration of war. In December 1941, the attack on Pearl Harbor gave the United States

SOURCE. Patrick C. T. White, *A Nation on Trial: America and the War of 1812* (New York: John Wiley & Sons, Inc., 1965), pp. 126–130. Reprinted by permission of the publisher.

no choice but to defend herself at once and with all her energy. These were clear-cut instances in which national agreements existed and governments would have been brought down had they not acted as they did. But if there was a consensus in 1812, it was not unanimous. And such as it was, it had been a long time in coming. Henry Adams said that the grounds for war, though strong in 1812, were weaker than they had been in June 1808 or January 1809. Why, then, did the declaration come when it did? The answers to this question have been diverse and even contradictory. Historians Alfred T. Mahan, Henry Adams, and A. L. Burt have emphasized the conflict over maritime rights. They have suggested that the disputes over impressment, the Orders in Council, and to a lesser extent paper blockades, contraband, and the Rule of 1756 were so insoluble that war was bound to come. Others, such as Louis Hacker and Pratt, were concerned with what appeared to be the highly sectional nature of the vote and sought their answers in land hunger or anger over Indian depredations committed on frontier settlements. Taylor saw regional forces at work, too, but argued that it was economic distress in the South and West, brought on by the Orders in Council, that drove these areas to war. More recently, Reginald Horsman and Bradford Perkins have stressed the complicated nature of the war's origins. The European wars created problems for America that were unexpected and difficult of solution. More perceptive diplomacy might have saved the situation, but, as Perkins suggests, Madison and Jefferson never rose to the heights that the crisis demanded.

The divided views on the causes of the war reflect, in part, the confusion existing in the country itself in 1812. But perhaps too much attention has been focused upon regional, sectional, and economic differences. The challenge to America was shared by all her citizens; the major differences arose over the means and methods for dealing with them. There can be no doubt that America's problems sprang from Europe's wars. In 1794 Jay's Treaty settled a number of grave Anglo-American differences. But it did not resolve the maritime disputes that were becoming increasingly serious. These were temporarily shelved when peace came in 1801, but they burst forth with greater force with the renewal of the struggle in 1803. From then until 1812 the United States was faced with practices which directly challenged her honor and her position. British impressment on the high seas affected Americans directly and emotionally. The insistence by London that Britain had the right to the services of all British subjects and the duty to secure these, even if it meant searching American ships in international waters, was bound to be dangerous. If impressment were deemed absolutely necessary to Britain's survival—and rightly or wrongly it was—then it was also properly considered to be a challenge to American sovereignty. If the flag of the United States could not protect her citizens, of what use was it? The Revolution had been fought for independence, and now independence was being threatened again.

What was true of impressment was also true of the Orders in Council. The government in London considered these decrees to be absolutely essential to the fight against Napoleon. Admittedly they also served British commercial interests in their struggle with American competitors and this consideration was taken into account when they were drafted. The United States could not help but see them as damaging to her economy and to her freedom. The general rights of neutrals to trade freely during wartime were widely recognized in the late eighteenth and early nineteenth centuries, and the new British doctrines of blockade and economic control were an affront to America. The enforcement of the Rule of 1756, the disputes over "free ships, free goods" and over broken and continuous voyages simply added to the simmering discontent in Washington. When an economic depression wasted large portions of the country and when Indian unrest threatened its borders, the simmering discontent boiled over into demands for war. The actions of France, too, harmed America. But France did not control the high seas as did Britain nor was she vulnerable to pressure through Canada, as was England. Further, though Naopleon might seize American ships, he frequently did it under the guise of municipal regulations. These facts were well understood by Jefferson who wrote that "France has kept pace with England in iniquity of principle, although not in the power of inflicting wrongs on us." If the roles of Britain and France had been reversed, who can doubt that America would have gone to war with Napoleon.

The challenge faced by Jefferson and Madison was the most serious since the winning of independence. Madison had no illusions about the extent or gravity of the situation. Soon after the war started he wrote:

"When the U.S. assumed & established their rank among the Nations of the Earth, they assumed & established a common

Sovereignty on the high seas, as well as an exclusive sovereignty within their territorial limits. The one is as essential as the other to their Character as an Independent Nation. However conceding they may have been on controvertible points, or forbearing under casual and limited injuries, they can never submit to wrongs irreparable in their kind, enormous in their amount, and indefinite in their duration; and which are avowed and justified on principles degrading the U. States from the rank of a sovereign and independent Power.

This was the heart of the matter. The sovereignty of the state itself was at stake. And when this was recognized, regional and sectional interests paled into insignificance. The challenge was to every American, and the preservation of the nation required that all muster to the flag. Recognition of the problem did not mean that its solution would be easy. Britain was fighting for her life and was not much concerned with legal niceties and international fictions. She would use force when it suited her purpose. Gradually Americans understood that this force would have to be answered by force. The United States was slow in coming to this understanding not because Jefferson was pacific in nature or because Madison could not screw up his courage to the testing point. Rather it was because Britain was one of the great world powers, and prudence and good sense demanded that peaceful negotiations be exhausted before other measures were considered. In the years from 1803 to 1812 the United States made one attempt after another to secure relief from British and French practices. Every means, short of war, was tried—endless discussion, entreaties, and economic coercion. They all failed. Either American views were not successfully portrayed, or Britain did not care deeply enough about the United States. It was, of course, the latter. London would have preferred American friendship, but she would not buy it if the price was surrender of her maritime practices.

So it was that after nine years of futile bargaining the United States finally decided that war was better than submission. Unfortunately there were those in the country who felt that negotiations were still feasible or that the wrong enemy had been chosen or that the cost of battle would be too high. Some in Massachusetts said that the conquest of Canada "would afford no indemnification, if achieved, for the losses to which we should be exposed upon our unprotected seaboard and upon the ocean." Others, largely Federalist in allegiance, believed that Britain was the last hope of ordered and good government and that to attack her would betray these principles. They suggested that American diplomacy had failed in its duty and that Britain was not fully aware of the depth of American feeling on certain subjects. Perhaps they were right, but it is doubtful that better men could have secured more advantageous terms. London was in no mood to compromise as long as France was the enemy.

In any event, by June 1812, a majority in Congress had decided that America would have to fight in order to survive. How could a government hold up its head if it could not protect its citizens? How could the Republic itself (let alone the Republican party) continue to exist if it did not rise to the challenge? When Calhoun talked of a second war of independence, he was not far from the mark. A young country was on trial. Its test would be whether it could survive in the harsh world of reality. That it did so under the leadership of a President who lacked both the imagination and the capacity to fire the enthusiasm of his countrymen said much for its intrinsic strength.

PART THREE

Peace and the Postwar Settlement

1 FROM *Raymond Walters, Jr.*
Albert Gallatin: Jeffersonian Financier and Diplomat

After three years of war the United States and Great Britain signed a peace treaty bringing an indecisive war to a close. Both sides had concluded that victory was unattainable. Certainly, it was quite clear by 1814 that the United States could not occupy Canada and that Britain could not inflict a total defeat on the American forces. Furthermore, domestic pressure for a settlement was strong. Britain was weary from twenty years of fighting, and the United States was torn by internal dissent. But while the desire for peace was strong, attaining it was difficult. Each side advanced unrealistic terms. Britain wanted a huge Indian neutral state carved out of American territory. America demanded an end to all the maritime practices which had so injured her as well as access to the fisheries in British North America which had been opened to her by the Treaty of 1783. A compromise had to be reached. On Christmas Eve in 1814 a treaty was signed which simply provided for a return to conditions as they had been before the outbreak of the war. Raymond Walters, Jr., in his Albert Gallatin, *gives a lucid and balanced picture of the negotiations that led to the Treaty of Ghent.*

THE TREATY OF GHENT

For quality and variety of talents, the five-man commission that entered the Hôtel des Pays Bas early on the afternoon of August 8, 1814, is unsurpassed in the history of American diplomatic relations. Ablest of the group in the long, tedious negotiations was

SOURCE. Raymond Walters, Jr., *Albert Gallatin: Jeffersonian Financier and Diplomat* (New York: The Macmillan Company, 1957; Pennsylvania: The University of Pittsburgh Press, 1969), pp. 276–288. Reprinted by permission of the author.

Albert Gallatin. This was the first time he had ever represented his adopted land internationally, and, through the spite of the Senate, his name was last instead of first among the commissioners. But at fifty-three he was the eldest and was the ripest in experience with men. He combined a thorough understanding of American temperament and aspirations and an instinctive comprehension of the ways of European courts that reminded perceptive men of Benjamin Franklin. His calmness, his tact, his reasoned judgment had already impressed his colleagues; his intense application to detail and his unquestioned devotion to his country were to awe them as the days passed.

Nominal head of the commission was John Quincy Adams, just forty-seven, who had lived much of his life abroad as secretary to his father and as a diplomat in his own right. His intellect as well as his experience qualified him for international negotiation; his personality did not. He once described himself as "a man of reserve, cold, austere, and forbidding manners."

Ten years younger and—on the surface—temperamentally a world apart was the tall, lanky Kentuckian, Henry Clay. He radiated charm, talked brilliantly, told salty stories, played cards and gambled, and pursued ladies zealously; but, when crossed, he entered into towering rages and brandished a sharp tongue. Clay had come to Ghent to find an acceptable end for a war he had done much to start, and to forward his ambition ultimately to become President. In Gallatin's view, his "great fault" was "that he is devoured with ambition."

Gallatin's almost constant companion of fifteen months, James A. Bayard, nicknamed "Chevalier" by his colleagues, was counted on to represent the Federalist view at the peace table; of the group, he was coolest and most even-tempered; he was a solid man, able, though far from brilliant. Least known and least capable of the Americans was Jonathan Russell, a career diplomat who was merely competent and a hypersensitive man. Russell was fascinated by Clay but held himself aloof from his other colleagues.

The three British commissioners were no match for these men. The one claim to fame of James, Baron Gambier, a handsome, white-haired admiral, was that he had commanded the fleet that bombarded the defenseless city of Copenhagen in 1807. Henry Goulburn was a rather reserved young man of thirty who had displayed a particular knowledge of Canadian affairs while serving as Under Secretary for the Colonies and War. A scholarly element was introduced by Dr. William Adams, a specialist in maritime law who was not without wit, and was fated to make a career of supernumerary roles.

At the outset the Britons received the Americans with a surprising cordiality. They were merely carrying out Castlereagh's instructions to sound out their adversaries' general attitude, to report back to London, and await further instructions. The truth was that Castlereagh considered them as messenger boys. The Americans might talk and write to Gambier, Goulburn, and Adams, but they were actually coping with Castlereagh, one of the greatest foreign ministers in British history; with Lord Bathurst, able Secretary for the Colonies and War; and with the Duke of Wellington, England's greatest soldier.

At dinner after the civilities of the first day's meeting, the Americans received two dispatches from Secretary Monroe, which significantly modified their instructions. They had been written in late June, at a dark hour in American history. The British were landing to raid Maryland and Washington; an army under General Sir George Prevost was headed to Canada, for an invasion of the United States by way of Lake Champlain. Monroe authorized the commissioners to postpone the subject of impressment, and even to omit it from their negotiations if that would bring the war to a prompt end. This would be abandonment of the issue that had taken the United States—officially at least—into war; but Gallatin had already advised this course, and he was of course pleased by the instructions.

Some of Gallatin's satisfaction wore off in the next two meetings, as the gulf between the two groups became clear. Monroe had instructed his negotiators to avoid discussion of the fishing privileges in Canada granted to Americans under the Treaty of 1783; Goulburn announced that these could not be "renewed" unless the British received an equivalent advantage. Monroe had directed the American commissioners to investigate definitions of blockade and the question of neutral rights; the British had been directed to shun these questions. Castlereagh had told his mouthpieces to make Indian "pacification" and Indian boundaries a *sine qua non* for peace; about these, the Americans had no instructions whatsoever.

When the British made plain this last object, the depression of the American commissioners deepened. It meant nothing less than creation of a buffer state between the United States and British holdings in North America. Both Americans and British were to be barred forever from purchasing land in the area, although the Indians might sell to others. Thus Castlereagh hoped to halt the transcontinental expansion of the American people. Adams and Bayard tried their hands at reporting this disturbing news, but it took Gallatin's judicious and careful touch to rewrite the report to the satisfaction of all. It was forwarded to America on August 18. The two commissions next faced each other on the morning of August 19 at the Chartreux, a former monastery where the British had taken up residence. During the interval the British commissioners had received a brief visit from Castlereagh himself en route, with an extensive retinue, to the European peace conference at Vienna. He left a new set of instructions and some fresh admonitions with his puppets.

The Americans, remembering that Monroe's first instructions had called for the cession of all Canada to the United States, listened in pained silence as Goulburn read from Castlereagh's new directions. The Indian boundary set up by the Treaty of Greenville in 1795 was to become the permanent boundary between British America and the United States. Thus American settlement would be blocked forever northwest of a line from Cleveland to the vicinity of Louisville, Kentucky. The Canadian frontier was to be "rectified" by assignment of Fort Niagara and Sackett's Harbor to the British. The United States was to be prohibited forever from maintaining naval forces or land fortifications on the Great Lakes.

Gallatin pressed for further details. In what he thought "overbearing language" and a "peremptory tone," the British agreed that they did not seek any cession of land to Canada except a small section of Maine to be used for a military road to connect Halifax and Quebec. The northwestern boundary was to be adjusted to permit British navigation of the Mississippi; this treaty right was to be continued forever.

Was the Indian barrier still to be considered as a *sine qua non?* "Certainly." What, asked Gallatin, was to become of the American citizens—perhaps a hundred thousand—already settled beyond the Greenville line, in the state of Ohio and the territories of Indiana, Illinois, and Michigan? They would have to shift for themselves, said Dr. Adams.

Morosely the Americans returned to their lodgings to frame a reply. Only Clay, the gambler and card player, observed that Castlereagh might be bluffing. Once again the final draughtsmanship fell to Gallatin, who insisted that "every expression that may be offensive" to the British be struck out. As transmitted on August 25, the note insisted, in firm and dignified style, that the establishment of an Indian boundary was not warranted by any principle of reciprocity, maxim of public law, or maritime right of the British. The surrender of "the rights of sovereignty and of soil of over one-third of the territorial dominions of the United States to a number of Indians, not probably exceeding twenty thousand" would be "instantaneously rejected" by Washington if the commissioners were so foolish as to forward the proposal. The other British demands "were above all dishonorable to the United States, in demanding from them to abandon territory and a portion of their citizens; to admit a foreign interference in their domestic concerns, and to cease to exercise their natural rights on their own shores and on their own waters."

The Americans sadly supposed that this would terminate the negotiation. Gallatin, Bayard, and even Clay planned to embark for home at a French port after another visit to Paris. Then from the Chartreux came word that their note was being referred to London. Would they please be patient for an answer? Gallatin and his colleagues of course could not guess it, and even the puppets in the Chartreux were in the dark; but Castlereagh had decided to stall for time. Soon Prevost and his forces would be moving south into New York State, winning by arms what he sought in North America. It would be a simple matter to demand *uti possidetis* at the peace table.

The next delaying action reached the Americans on September 5, in a memorandum sixteen folio pages long. Goulburn and his fellow commissioners elaborated their reasons for demilitarizing the Great Lakes and changing the Maine boundary. They flung out striking accusations: The United States was bent on aggrandizement in Florida, in Louisiana, and in the Indian territories. "It is notorious to the whole world that the conquest of Canada, and its permanent annexation to the United States, was the declared object of the American Government."

The Americans, meeting through an entire afternoon, read over the memorandum with mounting outrage, all the more bitter because they knew in their hearts that the charges contained an element of truth. But they could and did sputter at the phrase "the declared object"; never had the American government publicly admitted that it sought to acquire Canada. Clay, the avowed expansionist, contended that the note ought to be answered with

half a page. Gallatin undertook to analyze the contents and propose a reply. The others readily agreed.

For the next four days the group labored, singly and in conference. Gallatin prepared his analysis and submitted the draft of a
reply. In the light of the criticism it received, he revised his draft.
Adams tried his hand at a version; the others studied both forms,
commented, suggested. Adams later recorded that the finished work
was principally that of Gallatin and himself, the others merely
"altering, erasing, and adding": of what Gallatin wrote, approxi-
mately half was finally approved, only an eighth of his own composition being accepted. He believed that this was because Gallatin's
work was "argumentative," his own "declamatory."

The American note, as long as the one it answered, politely but
firmly denied that acquisition of Canada was an "avowed object,"
or that the United States had sought to acquire land by any but
peaceful means. It scored the British for encouraging the Indians
to attack American settlements and declared that, as the Maine
boundary was not at issue, the commissioners had not been
authorized to treat about it.

Eleven days passed. On September 20, Adams came to Gallatin's
apartment with a reply he had just received. The two scanned it
rapidly, then summoned the full commission. In what seemed to the
group an "overbearing and insulting" tone, the British reply
rejected the denial of imperialistic aims on the part of the United
States and enclosed copies of proclamations issued in the field by
Generals Smyth and Hull to support the charges in respect to
Canada. Although the note in effect abandoned most of the *sine qua
non* position previously taken, all the commissioners were dejected
by it.

Again Gallatin received the task of framing a reply. Adams
wished to include a reference to the "religious and moral duty" of
the United States to cultivate lands held by the Indians, but Gallatin
gently brushed this aside as likely to invite ridicule. After four
days of discussion and rewriting, the group had agreed upon a note
forthrightly reiterating the denial of American ambition for aggrandizement, and emphasizing that the proclamations of the
generals in Canada were no more an official expression of the
American government than that issued by the British admiral
during the *Chesapeake* affair. The note insisted that the United
States had always granted the Indians an equivalent for land taken
from them, and denied that violation of the Treaty of Greenville by

some of the Indians made it void. It admitted that the United States desired "to reclaim from the state of nature, and to bring into cultivation every portion of the territory within their acknowledged territories," and suggested that all nations, including Great Britain, should rejoice at the sight of a growing country and should reject the idea of a "perpetual desert" anywhere.

During the anxious days that followed the dispatching of this note on September 26, Adams, the nominal chief and a man little given to praise, realized that Gallatin, by his knowledge and manner, had in effect become the head of the delegation. "Mr. Gallatin keeps and increases his influence over us all," he wrote to his wife. "For extent and copiousness of information, for sagacity and shrewdness of comprehension, for vivacity of intellect, and fertility of resource," he thought his colleague was without peer in either the British or American delegations. He noted that, whenever a dispute had arisen over a particular paragraph in the discussion of a note, the majority had always supported Gallatin. He acknowledged that Gallatin had "more pliability of character and more playfulness of disposition" than himself, and so "throws off my heat with a joke." One day, when he got into an argument with Gallatin and Bayard over whether the Indian question should be considered as a *sine qua non*, Gallatin smiled and "in a tone of perfect good humor" told him that his argument was a *non sequitur*. "This turned the edge of the argument into mere jocularity," Adams recorded in his journal.

The British Under Secretary Goulburn was impressed more by Gallatin than by any of his fellows, but for different reasons. He believed that Gallatin alone comprehended the strong public opinion in England against making an "unsatisfactory" peace. "This," he told Bathurst, "perhaps arises from his being less like an American than any of his colleagues."

With the news that was dribbling into Ghent, Gallatin's even temper and jocular sallies were little short of heroic. The last week in September brought reports of severe military defeats. George Boyd, Adams's brother-in-law, arrived with a packet of letters that pointed up the desperation of the American government. One from Secretary of the Treasury Campbell, dated August 1, asked Gallatin to attempt to negotiate a $6,000,000 loan in Europe, preferably with the Amsterdam firm of Willinks. Gallatin promptly wrote to the Dutch bankers to sound them out.

On October 1 came the most awful news of all, borne by several persons who had read or heard reports in English newspapers about the "destruction of Washington" on August 24 and 25 by British forces. The next day Gallatin received a London journal giving the official British account of the burning of the Capitol, the President's house, and other public buildings. It was weeks before he learned that his own house on Capitol Hill had been burned by the invaders, although his furniture and other possessions, except for a box of valuable maps, had been saved. On October 14 the British commissioners deepened the mortification of the Americans by sending them copies of *The Times* reporting additional reverses at Machias and Passamaquoddy Bay, at Michilimackinac, and near Plattsburg.

Gallatin bore his grief and rage with reasonable calmness. But when Madame de Staël wrote from Paris for advice as to how to dispose of her holdings in American lands and stocks, his love for his adopted land overburst his reserve. The destruction of the Capitol and the Presidential mansion, he told her, was "an act of vandalism" unparalleled in twenty years of war in Europe; the British had committed it because, with the exception of certain cathedrals, England had no public buildings to compare with them. He advised her to hold on to her American property: the United States, he insisted proudly, always made good on national obligations.

As if to mock his loyalty, the Willinks a few days later advised Gallatin against trying to float a loan "at this time" in view of "the late untoward circumstances and the fear of what may further happen." When Crawford wrote that the same views were held at Paris, he reluctantly abandoned the attempt to obtain money.

Writing to Secretary Monroe about his decision, the old fire chief could not resist giving advice as to how the conflagration ought to be fought. No more stock ought to be issued than was absolutely necessary, and none at an interest rate higher than 8 per cent; taxes, especially indirect taxes, ought to be increased; the issue of Treasury notes should be carefully restricted; a new Bank of the United States should be chartered if politically practicable; public lands should be disposed of through a lottery. He was about to make suggestions concerning the raising of a militia, but checked himself: "I perceive that my zeal carries me out of my sphere."

The Americans had expected that the disaster at Washington would breed British truculence; but the note delivered late in the afternoon of October 8 was even more arrogant than they had feared. It made menacing references to the legality of the Louisiana Purchase: the King of Spain had been deprived of his proper role in the negotiations and had protested at the time; Great Britain had never been fully informed of the conditions of the sale. It again commented darkly on "aggrandizement" in the Floridas and offered assurances that the land the British sought in Maine was through unsettled areas. The most irritating feature of the note was an "ultimatum"; both nations must agree to the elimination of the Indian tribes as a factor in the war and to the restoration to them of all "possessions, rights, and privileges" they had enjoyed before the start of the war—or the negotiations would cease at once.

During the long discussion on the next day, most of the commissioners agreed with Gallatin that the ultimatum would have to be accepted. Public opinion in the United States, especially in New England, would not support continuance of the war on that issue alone. More important, if negotiations were broken off now, it would require months to arrange a resumption of peace talks. For two days Gallatin labored on an answer along these lines, which he presented to his colleagues on October 12.

Now Henry Clay took the initiative. Overnight he did a new draft, thoroughly characteristic of the man: brisker and more direct than the notes Gallatin and Adams had composed. This agreed to the Indian pacification provided peace were negotiated without delay. It proposed that the British transmit a list of all the points they thought imperative in a peace treaty and promised that the Americans would reply promptly in kind. The entire commission agreed to this, Adams most reluctantly.

The answer, like the note before it the work of Lord Bathurst, arrived on October 22. Bathurst shied away from Clay's proposal that the points at issue be stated; he insisted that the British had revealed their aims at the first meeting on August 8. His government was now willing to discuss or not, as the Americans pleased, naturalization and impressment. He proposed the same settlement in the Northwest that the two governments had tentatively agreed upon in 1803; elsewhere, settlement on the basis of *uti possidetis*. He would now deny Americans access to the unsettled shores in Canada for drying and curing of fish—a privilege granted under the Treaty of 1783.

Reading this note, the Americans angrily concluded that the British were still stalling for time, hoping for further gains in America that they might retain on the basis of *uti possidetis*. Actually, as the Foreign Office's archives revealed when they were opened years later, the note represented a considerable retreat by the British. In the past they had claimed about half of Maine and the land on the south side of the St. Lawrence from Plattsburg to Sackett's Harbor. Now they sought only the exclusion of American fishermen from Canada and a right of way to Halifax. They had been persuaded to these concessions because they had just learned of British military reverses in North America.

The Americans were of course quite in the dark as to all this and sought only to keep the negotiations alive. Gallatin drafted the reply that tersely reiterated their refusal to treat on the basis of *uti possidetis* or any principle involving cession of American territory; at the end of hostilities all territory captured by either side must be restored. Great Britain had not proposed a project for a treaty; the note therefore suggested that each nation submit one simultaneously. The note went to the British on October 26. To avoid a delay Gallatin and Adams began to draw up a project for their side. Five days later came a new British note that merely deepened the Americans' conviction that the enemy was stalling for time: It stated that the British had no further proposals to make, and indicated they now awaited the American project.

For the next week and a half the five Americans worked like beavers, sometimes together, sometimes separately. There were sharp differences of opinion that occasionally flared into fiery exchanges. Should they call for a commission to settle the impressment issue after the cessation of hostilities, or should they remain silent on the subject? Gallatin favored silence, and his view prevailed.

Over two issues—the right of Americans to fishing privileges in Canada and the right of the British to navigate the Mississippi freely —the words were even harsher. Clay, the spokesman of the West, wanted to deny access to the river, while Adams was anxious to preserve the fishing privileges on which much of New England's prosperity rested. Both rights were guaranteed in the Treaty of 1783. The British contended that, with the outbreak of the War of 1812, the treaty had ceased to be in effect—and their contention placed in doubt the very independence and sovereignty of the United States. When Gallatin suggested that both issues be referred to a commission for adjudication after the war, Clay paced up and down the chamber, shouting that he would not sign such a proposal.

The project that went to the British on November 10, composed by Gallatin, was an amalgam of the views of all his colleagues. The Mississippi was left unmentioned, and an accompanying note explained that the Americans were not authorized to discuss the fisheries question. It was proposed that the boundary issues be submitted to commissioners for settlement after the war, that the Indians be "pacified" by restoration to their 1811 status, that each nation assume responsibility for restraining the Indians in its territory. Perhaps the most important point was an insistence that at the end of hostilities each country must restore to the other land taken during the war.

Weeks now passed while both groups awaited word from London. During the interval they enjoyed themselves socially. With the exception of Adams, the Americans attended performances of a company of indifferent French actors and some fairly good especially enthusiastic attendants, and became frequent visitors backstage. There were parties and balls of various sizes and types, which even Adams attended. Gallatin bantered with him about the attention he was paying to the ladies, and assured the fair creatures that Adams's demonstrations were purely Platonic. Adams rejoined that Gallatin should pay court to the ladies in his own way, and he would do the same.

The people of Ghent, it developed, had grown weary of the British musical airs that had become a standard feature in the city, and inquired, through their musicians, whether the Americans had a national anthem. To their embarrassment, the guests of the Hôtel d'Alcantara discovered that none of them could sing or play "Hail Columbia." But Peter, Gallatin's Negro servant, could whistle it. So, while Peter whistled, a musician wrote it down; the piece was orchestrated, and thereafter at parties and public functions it was played as "l'air national des américains à grand orchestre."

Meanwhile the Americans received some heartening news. A dispatch from Secretary Monroe directed a firm hold on the principle of *status ante bellum* in respect to territory—an indication that the Administration was beginning to feel secure again. A ray of hope was shed on the government's financial situation by the appointment of Gallatin's friend A. J. Dallas to replace the inept Campbell in the Treasury. American newspaper accounts of the commissioners' first meetings in August, at which the British had disclosed their harsh demands, had rallied most of the Federalists and the lagging Democratic-Republicans behind the war effort.

Even British public circles echoed indignation when accounts of the meetings were printed in the London newspapers. For a day or two Gallatin believed it likely that the British would break off the negotiations as a consequence. "If they do," he told Adams bitterly, "it will only relieve us from the humiliation of being kept here in attendance upon their insulting caprices and insidious tergiversations."

The fact was that things were not going well for the British government. Two months earlier Lord Liverpool, the Prime Minister, had confided to Castlereagh that he wished they were rid of the war. Trade was in the doldrums, and he feared that complaints would soon be made against continuing the property tax merely "for the purpose of receiving a better frontier for Canada." As the weeks passed, it appeared that the peace congress at Vienna was moving nowhere—except possibly to a renewal of the European war. Anxious to liquidate the American war, Liverpool approached Britain's great military hero, the Duke of Wellington, who was serving as ambassador to Paris, with the proposal that he lead a great military force to America in the spring. At first Wellington acquiesced; but as he learned more about the military situation across the Atlantic he grew increasingly reluctant. Moreover, he told the cabinet members bluntly, Britain had no right to demand any cession of American territory. The cabinet determined to make peace as soon as practicable.

Gallatin's first intimation of a British change of heart was in letters from Alexander Baring in the third week of November. The London banker hoped that before the next payment of interest on Louisiana stock became due in January "some favourable change may occur." Ironically he had developed moral scruples against "advancing sums for the service of a government with which we are at war." The change of heart was made even clearer November 27 by a seemingly casual phrase in a note to the American commissioners. The British delegates wrote, "The undersigned have foreborne to insist upon the basis of *uti possidetis*, to the advantage of which they consider their country fully entitled."

This was cheering. However, the comments by the British in the margins of the Americans' November 10 project for a treaty, which they now returned, made it plain that other issues remained as much in the air as ever. More days of spirited debate about the fisheries and the Mississippi followed in the chambers of the Hôtel d'Alcantara. Gallatin argued that to abandon the fisheries would only strengthen the New England disunion movement. Clay exploded that it was foolish to try to conciliate a people who would not be conciliated, and at any rate the Mississippi ought to be closed to the British. In the end, Gallatin's calm tact won the Kentuckian over. They agreed that the American objective should be a *quid quo pro*: American use of the fisheries in return for British use of the Mississippi.

During these discussions it occurred to the Americans that it might be well to meet the British delegates again face to face. They made such a proposal by letter on November 30, and it was accepted within hours. Conferences were held on December 1, 10, and 12, alternating between the Chartreux and the Hôtel d'Alcantara. Each meeting lasted two to three hours, and each time the same old points were quibbled over anew. But by December 11 Gallatin was convinced that the British government desired peace heartily, and that the stage was being set for a genuine proffer of peace as soon as the sign was given in London.

With success apparently in the offing, Gallatin and Bayard persuaded Adams and Clay to drop their concern for the fisheries and the Mississippi; and on December 14 the Americans sent to the Chartreux a note expressing readiness to sign a treaty which would provide that all differences still unsettled would be negotiated later, with the understanding that there was no abandonment of any right previously claimed. The next eight days were agonizing for the Americans, because virtually the same proposal on November 10 had been rejected.

A British messenger put the reply into Gallatin's hands late on December 22, and he conferred at once with his colleagues. The British agreed to omit the article dealing with the fisheries and the Mississippi, but insisted that the islands that they held in Passamaquoddy Bay should continue in their possession until a three-man commission, composed of a friendly sovereign, an American, and a Briton, decided to whom they properly belonged.

This proposal to by-pass the fisheries and the Mississippi without a restatement of the Americans' claims irritated several members of the quintet at the Hôtel d'Alcantara, especially the volatile Clay. The "unseasonable trifling" of the Kentuckian exasperated Gallatin, and he told him so. The argument was resolved by a decision to propose yet another conference with the British, Clay alone stubbornly voting against the idea.

The British agreed to come to the Hôtel d'Alcantara for another meeting. The eight commissioners met for three hours the next afternoon and quibbled only over details, discovering somewhat to their surprise that the main outlines of a treaty had been agreed upon through their weeks of exchanges. An overnight recess. Then, on the afternoon before Christmas, 1814, from four o'clock to half-past six, they reconvened at the Chartreux, carefully read and compared the six copies of the document, and affixed their signatures. Gallatin's was the last of the eight. Adams voiced the hope of all his colleagues that this would be the last treaty of peace that need ever be signed between Britain and the United States.

Actually, the 2,250 words of the treaty, over which they had labored for almost five months, did no more than state that everything was to be as it had been at the time of the American declaration of war. The impressment issue, the declared purpose of the war was not mentioned; the other moot questions were to be settled by commissioners to be appointed later. The important thing had been to obtain peace at once, and that had been accomplished. Gallatin expressed his own feeling on Christmas Day, when he wrote to Secretary Monroe, more in relief than in triumph, that the treaty was "as favorable as could be expected under existing circumstances, as far as they were known to us."

In other ways, time was to prove the treaty of value to both countries. It resolved a political and military stalemate and marked a turn for the better of relations that had been steadily deteriorating for a decade and a half. It allowed the United States to turn to the determination of its own destiny on the American continent, freed from fears of British designs to create a neutral Indian barrier state and of British conspiracies with Indians within its borders. White settlement was speeded in the Old Northwest, and the ultimate opening of the Far West was hastened. At the same time, the treaty allowed Britain to concentrate on coping with changing trade conditions throughout the world.

It was John Quincy Adams's painfully honest opinion that Gallatin had made the largest and most important contribution to the conclusion of the peace at Ghent. Gallatin's contribution was not simply calm determination and tactful patience; it was even more his national view of the interests of the United States, contrasting so sharply with the regional views of the Yankee Adams and the westerner Clay.

This national feeling permeated an assessment of the War of 1812 that Gallatin sent to an old friend not long after: "The war has been productive of evil and good, but I think the good preponderates. Independent of the loss of lives, and the losses of property by individuals, the war has laid the foundation of permanent taxes and military establishments, which the [Democratic-Republicans] had deemed unfavorable to the happiness and free institutions of the country. But under our former system we were becoming too selfish, too much attached exclusively to the acquisition of wealth, above all too much confined in our political feelings to local and state objects. The war has renewed and reinstated the National feelings and character which the Revolution had given, and which were daily lessened. The people now have more general objects of attachment with which their pride and political opinions are connected. They are more American: they feel and act more as a Nation, and I hope that the permanency of the Union is thereby better secured."

2 FROM *Samuel Flagg Bemis*
John Quincy Adams and the Foundations of American Foreign Policy

The Treaty of Ghent brought the War of 1812 to a close, but it did not resolve all of the issues that divided Britain and the United States. The most pressing of these involved the fisheries and the western boundary. Great Britain insisted that the declaration of war in 1812 had terminated the agreement in the Treaty of 1783 which had given Americans the liberty to fish in certain Canadian waters. The United States insisted that the war had only suspended these privileges and that the return of peace meant an automatic restoration of the fisheries' clauses of the treaty. In addition to this vexatious problem there was the question of the boundary west of the Lake of the Woods. Both of these potentially dangerous questions were settled by the Convention of 1818. Under its terms the Americans were given the liberty to fish in certain specified Canadian waters while the boundary was drawn west of the Lake of the Woods along the 49° parallel to the Rocky Mountains. The Oregon territory was left open to nationals of both countries. This "joint occupation" was ultimately to become as explosive as a time bomb, and the question of final ownership was not resolved before relations between both countries were strained to the breaking point. Professor S. F. Bemis, in his definitive study of John Quincy Adams, untangles the complicated negotiations which led to the settlement of 1818.

THE CONVENTION OF 1818

Already President Monroe's Administration had been seeking, through the instrumentality of Richard Rush, to build up an even broader-based settlement than that suggested by Castlereagh. The United States wanted a treaty that would do more than resolve these disputes which were, after all, only a minor matter for the British Government. Monroe and Adams wanted to put at rest the great and difficult problems of colonial commerce and the Freedom of the Seas. And Rush's original instructions, at Monroe's own impulse rather than with Adams's approval, had authorized him to put forward successive compromises for a settlement of the impressment

SOURCE. Samuel Flagg Bemis, *John Quincy Adams and the Foundations of American Foreign Policy*, pp. 287–299. Copyright 1949 by Samuel Flagg. Reprinted by permission of Alfred A. Knopf, Inc., and the author.

issue. The final offer was to exclude by statute all "native born British subjects" from American ships of war and merchant marine if Great Britain would formally give up the practice of impressment. Such was what the American Peace Commissioners had been originally instructed to propose in 1813. Such was what Adams himself had proposed in London in 1816 under instructions, but against his own better judgment.

The first British reaction was discouraging. When Rush presented his final proposal, in July 1818, the Conference of Aix-la-Chapelle was still some months in the future. Castlereagh admitted that such a law would be a "step forward," but declared that his Government was unwilling to meet it by giving up in any treaty, whatever its terms, the right of entering foreign vessels to look for British subjects. He did not, however, dismiss any further discussion of the subject. We shall see presently that he later came back to Rush's proposals. The Foreign Minister was even less encouraging on the American offer of complete reciprocity of commerce and navigation between the United States and British dominions in North America, including the West Indies; the British Government, he repeated, was not ready to abandon its colonial system. It would do no more than renew the limited Commercial Convention of July 3, 1815.

Adams had not heard fully the result of Rush's conversations with Castlereagh when, in response to the British proposals already made for a settlement of the issues of slaves, boundaries, and fisheries, he drew up, at the President's direction, instructions to a new diplomatic commission to make a general treaty of amity and commerce to settle all the issues between the two countries. The experienced Gallatin was ordered across the Channel to assist Rush in the negotiation.

From his own long experience in London, dating back to his first conversations with Lord Grenville in 1795, the Secretary had little expectation that Great Britain would concede anything on impressment or on the Freedom of the Seas. That being the case, he had no desire to embarrass the proposed commercial negotiation with questions of maritime regulations adapted to a state of warfare. He did not want to draw into further discussion such subjects as blockade, contraband trade with enemies or their colonies, or even impressment, unless such a wish should be manifested on the British side. In the latter case the Commissioners were to be governed by the instructions already issued to Rush.

Nor was there much hope, from the account of Rush's first conversation with Castlereagh, that Great Britain would accept complete reciprocity of trade in American and British vessels, on equal terms, between the United States and British dominions in North America, including the British West Indies. The independence of the United States had at least one advantage to British navigation: it had wiped out the competition of Yankee shipping in the carrying trade between England and the remaining colonies, and between the colonies themselves. In case of the expected refusal, the Secretary of State indicated that the United States would accept a renewal for a term of years of the very meager Convention of July 3, 1815. This was the treaty that Adams, Gallatin, and Clay had signed in London prohibiting reciprocally any discriminations against the citizens or subjects of either party in the direct trade between the United States and the United Kingdom. If necessary, said Adams, Monroe's Administration would accept this limited trade with the "old country" and abide as cheerfully as possible the result of a dubious and undesirable "experiment" of closing the doors against each other's flag in North America—a threat that the United States might exclude British ships coming from British colonies.

The only objection that Lord Castlereagh had been able to make to the proposed complete reciprocity of commerce between the dominions of each party in North America had been that the British colonial system had been "long established." Such a statement, felt Adams, was nothing more than the age-old argument of existing abuse against proposed reform. He might have added that it was most inconsistent. At the very moment that Great Britain was excluding the flag of the United States from the Atlantic ports of British North America and the West Indies she was insisting upon the entrance of British vessels into the ports of Spanish America, despite the existence for centuries of Spain's colonial monopoly.

Turning to other issues—slaves, the boundary west of the Lake of the Woods, and the settlement at the mouth of the Columbia River—the Secretary of State noted the willingness of the British Government to submit each of these questions to two-men joint commissions like the boundary commissions set up by the Treaty of Ghent. Castlereagh had suggested such a reference as a first step; then if two commissioners disagreed he would submit the controversy to the arbitration of a friendly sovereign, presumably the Emperor of Russia.

Adams was not willing to place in the uncertain channel of arbitration such immense territorial questions, so important to the continental future of the United States, so relatively insignificant for Great Britain. He quickly discovered serious objections to such procedure. The Czar also had pretensions to territory on the North West Coast. The territorial dispute, furthermore, was not analogous to the controversy over deported slaves that had arisen from opposing interpretations of the language of the first article of the Treaty of Ghent, on which the two Governments were still disagreed. The conflicting claims to the North West Coast did not involve the interpretation of a treaty. It was a matter of give and take. If compromise were the object, said Adams, it would be much better to reach it directly than to entrust the concessions to commissions supposed to be judicial in nature.

Thus by implication the Secretary of State left these three issues to be settled somehow by Gallatin and Rush but with admonitions that the utmost that the American Commissioners could offer on the boundary was the agreement that had been initialed back in 1807. That was the line of 49° westward from the Lake of the Woods as far as the respective territories *of the two parties* extended in that quarter, with exclusion from this formula of all the region west of the Rocky Mountains. Great Britain, insisted Adams, had no valid claim upon this Continent south of 49° N.L. But as a last stand he was willing to accept—what Monroe had always been willing to take—the line of 49° all the way through to the Pacific Ocean.

Next in hand came the fisheries. John Quincy Adams, in obedience to the President rather than by his own option, at last indicated the choice of shores for a perpetual liberty. He was careful to use language that did not disclaim the contention of John Adams and the Government of the United States throughout the controversy, that the War of 1812 had not terminated the fishery liberty. He was willing to desist from the liberty generally in return for a permanent right, good even against war, on stipulated coasts. It was another proposed compromise.

To secure the substance more or less without abandoning altogether the principle of contest, as circumstances may require, has always been the essence of Anglo-American appeasement: in Jay's Treaty of 1794, in the Treaty of 1818, in the Treaty of Washington of 1871, placing the *Alabama* claims in the way of settlement; in the War Claims Agreement of 1927. Now it has been one side, now the other, to which the principle was more important than the substance. In 1818 the substance was more important to the United States than the principle. But Adams strove for the honor of his

family as well as the consistency of his country to save the principle
too, or at least the shadow of it.

The British Government readily accepted the expanded negotiation. On the eve of his departure for Aix-la-Chapelle, Castlereagh
did everything personally and officially to expedite matters. He left
the actual labor to two of his subordinates who had signed the Convention of July 3, 1815: Henry Goulburn, also remembered for his
part at Ghent, and Frederick John Robinson, president of the
Board of Trade and now a member of the Cabinet. Both sides
quickly agreed to renew indefinitely the convention they had signed
three years before. Then they took up the issues of fisheries, northwest boundary, and deported slaves before they tackled the more
difficult problems of colonial commerce, the Freedom of the Seas,
impressment, and the slave trade. Each of these settlements or near
settlements deserves some particular notice.

Gallatin and Rush succeeded in getting an even more extensive
inshore fishing liberty than John Quincy Adams's instructions had
prescribed. The Secretary had demanded permanent rights on the
southern shore of Newfoundland and on the Labrador Coast. The
treaty secured them on the shores of the Magdalen Islands too. It
stipulated for the inhabitants of the United States the liberty "for
ever" in common with British subjects to take fish of every kind on
the following coasts, bays, harbors, and creeks of His Britannic
Majesty's Dominions in America: southern Newfoundland from
Cape Ray to Rameau Island, on the western and northern coast of
Newfoundland, from Cape Ray to the Quirpon Islands, on the
shores of the Magdalen Islands, and on the coasts of Labrador
indefinitely northward from Mount Joli, without prejudice to any
exclusive rights of the Hudson's Bay Company; also the liberty "for
ever" to dry and cure fish in any of the unsettled coasts of Labrador
as long as they remained unsettled. In return the United States re-
nounced any liberty to exploit the remaining inshore fisheries of
British North America.

What the British objected to during the negotiation was not at
all the stretches of coast demanded by the Americans, but rather
any language which would imply that the old liberty had not been
abrogated by the recent war, or that the newly granted liberty (as
Goulburn and Robinson preferred to construe it) would be safe
against a future war. The Americans on the other hand stuck to

John Quincy Adams's desire for phraseology expressing a survival of the old liberty. For the future they accepted a liberty "for ever" instead of an express provision, which they would have preferred, that the article could never be abrogated by war. The British strenuously resisted even these two words, but finally accepted them.

Whether such language will survive the effect of war on treaties doubtless will never be tested because of the good nature of Anglo-American relations since then. The fact remains that the American Commissioners in 1818 accepted a weaker phraseology on this point, even as John Adams in 1782 had tolerated the weaker word *liberty* instead of the absolute word *right* for the inshore fisheries. The language of the treaty saved to some degree the contentions and the honor of both and yielded the principal substance to the United States. It was another compromise.

In the discussions about the boundary the British Commissioners made a final effort to close the northwest gap by dropping the line from the Lake of the Woods down to the Mississippi and providing for (but not restoring—that would have been inconsistent with their fishery contention) the future navigation of the river from its source to the ocean. Finding that the American plenipotentiaries were forbidden by their instructions to accept any lowering of British territory to the latitude of the Mississippi, not to mention its free navigation, they readily agreed to extend the line of 49° N.L. westward to the Rocky Mountains. There they stopped.

Gallatin and Rush proposed to carry the line right straight through to the Pacific Ocean. Robinson and Goulburn declined this but intimated that they might take it a little farther along over the mountains, as far as the Columbia River, then down the great River of the West to salt water. Warned by their chief that Great Britain could have no valid claims on the Continent south of 49°— if indeed they needed such a warning—the American plenipotentiaries refused to yield. Then their British friends proposed to leave the region west of the mountains, and lying between 49° and 45°, free and open to the subjects and citizens of both states for the purpose of trade and commerce. Let it be agreed, they suggested, that neither would exercise against the other any sovereign or territorial authority, all without prejudice to any claim of either party or to the pretensions there of any other power. This would have cut the United States out of any worth-while claim to territory west of the mountains and north of 49°. It would have given to Great Britain at least as good a claim as the United States to what soon came to be known as the Oregon Country—that is, the Columbia River basin, Puget Sound, and the Olympic Peninsula. Gallatin and Rush refused to fall into this territorial trap. They contested Britain's claim to the region north as well as south of the line. They had been willing to accept the line of 49° only as a compromise.

Article III of the Treaty of 1818 finally agreed to leave the whole North West Coast of America, without mention of its boundaries north or south, "free and open, for the term of ten years . . . to the Vessels, Citizens, and Subjects of the Two Powers" without prejudice to the claims of either party, or to those of any other power or state, "the only object of the High Contracting Parties in that respect, being to prevent disputes and differences amongst Themselves." It was still another compromise prolonging the status quo, meanwhile agreeing quite peaceably to disagree. It left either party completely free to exercise acts of sovereignty within the disputed area.

Actually this article of the convention was a temporary waiver of discussion of sovereignty. Nobody expected it to set the question at rest, least of all Adams. "It will certainly come upon us again," he noted, "for which I ought to be prepared. Let me remember it."

There was no danger that he would forget it.

Lord Castlereagh's previous willingness to arbitrate the controversy over deported slaves led to a quick agreement. The two parties concurred in Article V of the Convention of 1818 to refer to some friendly sovereign or state—it proved to be the Czar of Russia—the question whether the true intent and meaning of the treaty of Ghent entitled the United States to the restitution of, or full compensation for, all of the slaves carried away. Subsequently they selected the Czar of Russia as the arbitrator and further conferred upon him the office of mediator in the negotiations that must ensue between them in consequence of the award they had requested. On April 22, 1822 Count Nesselrode handed down the Czar's opinion that the United States was entitled to indemnity. Under his mediation the United States and Great Britain signed a convention (June 30/ July 12, 1823) providing for two mixed commissions with umpires to sit at Washington (1) to fix the average value of each slave for which indemnity was due, and (2) to determine the number of slaves and other private property for which compensation must be paid.

The first mixed commission succeeded in performing its duty acceptably to both parties, but the second commission disputed and wrangled ineffectually. In 1826 the two Governments concluded a convention by which Great Britain agreed to pay to the United States the sum of $1,204,960 in full satisfaction of all obligations. Congress then had to set up an American commission to distribute the money to the claimants, finally completed in 1828.

This whole affair of securing "justice" for the slave-owners injured by loss of their human property took four years of patience and labor of John Quincy Adams as Secretary of State and President.

These important Anglo-American negotiations in London on the eve of the Conference of Aix-la-Chapelle came close to settling at least two of the unsolved issues that then stood in the way of a complete Anglo-American rapprochement: the question of reciprocal trade between the United States and the remaining British colonies of the New World, and the issue of impressment.

Goulburn and Robinson expressed a willingness to allow to American and to British vessels equally a direct commerce between the United States and the British West Indies in several important commodities of that trade, not however including sugar and coffee and specifically excluding salt provisions of all kinds. Not very preposterously they reserved for their Government a right to levy lower, preferential, duties on the allowed products when imported into the British West Indies from British North America in British ships, the only vessels that could legally engage in the intercolonial trade. They also planned that sugar and coffee would reach the United States only in British ships by way of Nova Scotia or New Brunswick. Despite these significant reservations the concession offered in the direct trade was a very considerable one. It would have opened an irreparable hole in the dike of mercantilism. As for trade between British North America and the United States, Goulburn and Robinson advanced no proposition for overland commerce or by inland waterways. All they offered was a limited reciprocity of maritime carriage of enumerated home products between the United States and the Maritime Provinces.

The American Commissioners did not consider the complicated British propositions to be real reciprocity within the meaning of their instructions. They saw at once how the articles were contrived to favor British intercolonial commerce carriage at the expense of American goods and ships. Nevertheless the two plenipotentiaries agreed to send the drafted articles along to their Government *ad referendum.* In his dispatches to John Quincy Adams on this point Gallatin dwelt on Robinson's persuasion that Great Britain was bound to recede further with the passage of time, that an unlimited intercourse (except perhaps in salt provisions) would be certain to follow these limited beginnings.

President Monroe referred the proposed British articles to the Senate. After careful consideration the newly established Committee on Foreign Relations made a confidential report which evidenced a willingness to go a long way toward meeting them—farther, indeed, than the Administration itself was willing to travel. Adams canvassed the complicated subject with at least two opposition Senators, Rufus King of New York, and Harrison Gray Otis of Massachusetts. King opposed it. Otis seemed to favor it. At the President's request he went over the matter with Crawford, Calhoun, and Attorney General Wirt. They finally agreed to instruct Rush to accept a reciprocity limited, as the British proposed, to the direct trade in enumerated articles; but only upon condition that the duties upon imported articles should not be higher when carried into the British West Indies from the United States than when similar articles were imported from other foreign countries *or from British colonies or dominions themselves.*

The Secretary of State embodied these requirements in two new articles to be added to those which the British Government had offered. The purpose was to give effect to reciprocity in fact as well as in words in such direct trade as might be opened up between the United States and the British West Indies. Adams and his colleagues hardly expected the British Government to abandon its sovereign right to intercolonial preferential duties. Nor did they think Britain would give up the right to exclude all foreign ships from the inter-colonial trade. Without such concessions, not unreasonable legally, real and effective reciprocity in the permitted articles of direct trade would be largely nominal. Favored by lower preferential duties, the acceptable commodities would flow back and forth between the United States and the West Indies in British ships through con-venient colonial vestibules in Quebec, New Brunswick, Nova Scotia, and Bermuda.

When Rush took up the subject again with Lord Castlereagh, he met the expected objections. Without hesitation Castlereagh de-clared that the American proposals were not of a nature to form the basis of any agreement between the two countries.

"They would effect," said the Foreign Minister, "an entire sub-

version of the British colonial system." He went on to describe that
system in language which echoed the eighteenth century. All this did
not slacken his efforts to subvert the whole Spanish colonial system
by insisting on freedom of trade for British subjects and ships in
all the ports and regions of South America.

Neither the American Revolution nor the revolution of the
Spanish colonies had yet taught their full lesson to the British Tory
Government. The United States on its part was not willing to take
half a cake of British West Indian trade. Both nations fell back on
their respective navigation laws. Most obstinately and unprofitably
they continued to exclude each other's ships from any commerce
between their possessions in the New World. The issue remained
for John Quincy Adams to struggle with in Anglo-American relations throughout the remainder of his administrative career.

On impressment, touchiest question of all, the British Government showed a surprising readiness to treat. At this particular juncture of world politics Lord Castlereagh on his own initiative had
brought up the subject in preliminary and informal conversations
with Rush before the arrival of Gallatin from Paris. He actually
offered, with two changes,. to accept the proposals that Rush had
made at the beginning of his mission: to abolish impressment, subject to an agreement by each party not to allow *henceforth* the natural-
born subjects or citizens of the other party to serve in its navy or
merchant marine. These were Castlereagh's two proposed modifications: (1) the treaty or convention to be limited to a term of years,
eight, ten, or twelve, with liberty to each party to denounce it upon
a notice of, say, three or six months; (2) "that the British boarding
officer, entering American ships at sea for a purpose justified under
the laws of nations, should have the liberty of calling for the list of
the crew, and, if he saw a seaman known to him, or on good
grounds suspected of being an Englishman, that he should have the
further privilege of making a record or *procès verbal* of the fact, in
such a way as to have the case distinctly brought under the attention
of our [i.e., the American] Government, though by no means with-
drawing the man from the ship."

The first proposed modification, the Foreign Minister observed to
Rush, would be a regulation to guard against any irrevocable relinquishment of the right of impressment, which British opinion "or
even prejudice" might not, after a trial, be willing to tolerate. The
second would operate as a further incentive to the faithful execution

by the United States of its domestic legislation for prohibiting the service of native-born British seamen.

Rush thought the first point unobjectionable, but objected strenuously to the second. "It comes as a first objection," he wrote to Secretary Adams, "and we may therefore hope to get rid of it altogether." With much elation he declared to his chief that at last the British Government seemed ready to abandon the ancient practice to which it had clung so long and so tenaciously. Anxiously he waited for Gallatin to join him to bring the work to a decision.

Once more the European situation came to the help of the United States. It should have made it possible to clear up the impressment issue altogether. At Aix-la-Chapelle, Castlereagh's chief anxiety would be to stem the efforts of Alexander I to transform the Quadruple Alliance from the specific purpose (as interpreted by Great Britain) of protecting the peace settlement of 1815 against another eruption of France, into the vague interventionist motives of the Holy Alliance. He also intended to appeal to the Christian professions of the legitimist monarchs of Europe to acknowledge a reciprocal right of visit and search of each other's merchant ships in time of peace for the suppression of the African slave trade. In reality this would have been tantamount to a mandate to the British Navy, which had so abused that right in time of war, particularly in the impressment of American seamen. Castlereagh did not want the powers of the Holy Alliance to find a possible supporter in the United States, too sorely rebuffed at his hands on the issue of impressment.

Just before his departure for the port of embarkation Castlereagh called Rush to his office. The American Minister found the Secretary's coach waiting to take him to a Channel port. Hastily the Foreign Minister announced the decision of his Government finally to accept the American proposal for the abolition of impressment and to waive the second suggested British modification. Proposals to that end, he promised, would be put into shape as soon as Rush and Gallatin were ready with theirs on the fisheries and the West Indies. "The great principle at last being settled," said Castlereagh warmly, "that on your engaging not to employ British seamen, we will cease to impress them from your vessels, I hope all details will be easily arranged." Castlereagh left for the European Congress hopeful that he need expect no embarrassments from the other side of the water.

The British Commissioners had submitted definite articles for a special treaty abolishing impressment during at least a term of years.

In doing so they had formally expressed their conviction that, with all the difficulties that surrounded the issue it should be sufficient to satisfy their American friends of the earnest disposition of Great Britain to go to every practicable length to connect the two countries in the firmest ties of harmony. The British draft treaty abolished impressment reciprocally on the "high seas" for a period of ten years. There were, however, some conditions attached. The treaty was terminable at any time after six months' notice; and it introduced a new proviso: nothing in the treaty should protect the vessels of either party which might find themselves in the ports or "maritime jurisdiction" of the other.

Gallatin and Rush made no objection to the time limits, or to the principle allowing impressment of subjects or citizens within the proper territorial waters of either party. They succeeded in adding the "narrow seas" to the "high seas" where impressment was to be prohibited. They further introduced the qualification "as acknowledged by the law of nations" after the words "maritime jurisdiction' to define the area where impressment was to be legal.

The British delegates promptly accepted these important amendments as well as minor verbal changes. But on the very threshold of success the negotiation stumbled fatally over small technical obstacles.

The second article of the proposed treaty provided that each party should draw up and deliver to the other within eighteen months following "signature" a list of all the naturalized seamen known to be in its maritime service at that date. Thenceforth no person whose name was not included in that list could claim the privileges of American citizenship under the treaty. The American negotiators explained in great detail that it would be impractical and impossible to get up a definitive list because of the previous deficiencies of their Federal and state registration laws. Therefore they reserved the right of any individual to show good proof of his former naturalization after the ratification of the treaty. Constitutional doubts over *ex post facto* legislation, doubts that seem today quite absurd, impelled them to insist that the list itself go into effect only at ratification of the treaty rather than from its signature. These objections quite absurdly convinced the British negotiators in their turn that there would be a big loophole for hordes of British seamen to naturalize themselves before the treaty went into effect. They refused to entertain the American reservations. So no special anti-impressment treaty was signed.

It seems a pity that the two Governments got so near to a settlement of the historic dispute only to fail so miserably. Had Gallatin and Rush signed the treaty, there is good reason to think that Monroe would have accepted it notwithstanding Adams's advice against agreeing to any treaty that would permit impressment in the future under any circumstances anywhere. Monroe had decided to accept the arrangement, subject to abrogation at four years' notice. Whether he would have agreed to Castlereagh's term of six months' notice remains a question. Six months' notice would have enabled Great Britain to throw off the prohibition of impressment soon after the beginning of the next war. If Monroe had accepted such a short term for the giving of notice to abrogate—a condition that went far to nullify the value of the American concession henceforth not to employ any native-born British subjects in the United States merchant marine—such a treaty would still have had to get the approval of two thirds of the Senate.

The four-point Treaty of 1818 (fisheries, slaves, boundaries, trans-Atlantic commerce) arrived in Washington without any settlement of the other major issues. With all its limitations it was a sturdy advancement of Anglo-American amity. No less an authority than Professor A. L. Burt has pronounced it the most important treaty in the history of Canadian–American relations.

The Senate promptly and unanimously ratified President Monroe's first treaty, negotiated under the direction of Secretary of State John Quincy Adams. For one thing it secured the fisheries, and that was due to the unremitting efforts and arguments of the Adamses, father and son. The father's success in preserving the inshore fisheries in 1782, albeit in equivocal language, the son's determination not to yield them at Ghent, and his later obstinate and resourceful insistence that the liberty lived on after the War of 1812 saved this valuable resource for their countrymen. The compromise of 1818 secured for New England fishermen a continued enjoyment to this day of the best inshore fisheries of British North America almost as if they were a part of the United States itself, and that without extending to British subjects reciprocally any liberty to fish within American territorial waters. *Piscemur, venemur, ut olim.* Thanks to John Adams and to John Quincy Adams, their fellow countrymen would fish and hunt as of yore.

The boundary articles were of even greater importance to the

United States. Article III by taking the boundary westward to the Rocky Mountains secured beyond any cavil of future doubt or challenge for the United States the northwestern part of Minnesota and most of North Dakota and Montana. It was a rich territory with room for homesteads for millions of American citizens and natural resources still uncalculated. The boundary settlement of 1818 further gave diplomatic momentum for carrying the line across to the Pacific Ocean. As the Republic grew westward in strength it was easily able, in 1827, to renew the article on the North West Coast (Article III) for another period of twenty years.

The Convention of 1818 was of great advantage to each party in the existing diplomatic situation. It enabled Great Britain to turn her attention to the European situation undistracted by the prospect of any trouble with the United States. It left Monroe's Government free to drive home its contemporaneous negotiation with Spain without fear of any difficulties with Great Britain. Even as he handed the British treaty to the President, John Quincy Adams was deep in diplomatic discussions with the Spanish Minister in Washington for a treaty that would carry the acknowledged southern boundary of the United States all the way across the Continent.

3 FROM   *A. P. Whitaker*

The United States and the Independence
of Latin America, 1800–1830

*The Convention of 1818 had defined a major portion of the northern boundary of
the United States, and the Louisiana Purchase had extended the southern dimensions
of America. But there were still major gaps to be filled and great uncertainties about
portions of the boundary. One of the most disturbing problems for any President was
the question of Florida. The possession of that area by any foreign power posed a continuous threat to the security of the United States. In 1810 West Florida was seized
by the Americans, but this still left East Florida in Spanish hands.*

*How to gain this area peacefully challenged President Monroe. Happily, circum-
stances came to his aid. The revolt of the Spanish American colonists distracted
Madrid. The incursions of General Jackson into Florida and the determined diplomacy
of Adams convinced Spain that this North American colony would ultimately fall into
the hands of the United States. Therefore she decided to negotiate its transfer to the
United States. By the Adams–Onís Treaty which was signed in 1819, America received
East Florida, and her seizure of West Florida validated, secured a definition of the
boundary of the Louisiana Territory, and gave up any shadowy claim which she might
have to Texas. Professor A. P. Whitaker has analyzed both the reasons and the importance of this highly advantageous treaty.*

THE ADAMS–ONÍS TREATY ON FLORIDA

If we may trust a report received through Gallatin, there was a
close connection between the Congress of Aix-la-Chapelle and the
surrender of Spain to the United States in the controversy over
Florida and other questions dating back to the period of the
Napoleonic wars. The details of this long-drawn-out negotiation
need not detain us here, for our only concern is with its bearing on
the movement for independence in Spanish America.

As is well known, Spain long refused to agree to any settlement
of the points at issue which was acceptable to the United States, and,

SOURCE. A. P. Whitaker, *The United States and the Independence of Latin America, 1800–
1830* (Baltimore: The Johns Hopkins Press, 1941), pp. 266–274. Reprinted by permission of the publisher.

as we have had occasion to observe, more than once in the years from 1815 to 1818 the controversy threatened to bring on a war between the two powers. Suddenly, late in 1818, the Spanish minister for foreign affairs, the Marqués de Casa Irujo, sent the Spanish plenipotentiary in the United States, Onís, instructions under which he negotiated with John Quincy Adams a treaty (signed February 22, 1819) conceding most of the points contended for by the United States. The latter was confirmed in the possession of the parts of Florida that it already held, and acquired the rest of that strategically important colony; gave up its claim to Texas but acquired Spain's claim to the territory on the Pacific coast north of the forty-second parallel (the Oregon country); and paid Spain five million dollars, which sum was ear-marked for the satisfaction of the spoliation claims of its own citizens against Spain.

The reasons for this sudden surrender by the Spanish court of a position that it had long maintained with great tenacity have been a subject of much study and speculation. For many years it was believed that Andrew Jackson's invasion of Florida early in 1818, skilfully exploited by Adams in his negotiation with Onís, was mainly responsible for Spain's decision to barter away a colony that she was in imminent danger of losing in any case. So many other factors and so many other issues besides Florida were involved, however, that this explanation would hardly seem adequate. Recent research has clarified this question, first, by confirming the belief that Jackson's invasion had "an electric effect" on the negotiation; second, by showing that Adams's exploitation of it in his famous despatch to Minister Erving at Madrid came too late to affect the course of the Spanish court; and third, by showing that the new head of the Spanish government, Irujo, hastened the conclusion of the negotiation with the United States in order to give Spain a free hand for the reconquest of its American colonies by means of the great expeditionary force which it was assembling at Cadiz at this time.

To one important question, however, no satisfactory answer has been given: what relation, if any, did the Spanish surrender to the United States bear to the failure of the determined effort that Spain made in 1818 to obtain the intervention of the great powers in its behalf in Spanish America?

Such an explanation is suggested by a despatch from Albert Gallatin which has not, so far as is known, come to the attention of previous students of this problem. Writing in May 1819 from

Paris, which was the diplomatic center of Europe and was in very close touch with Spain, Gallatin said:

"Marquis Dessole [the French minister of foreign affairs] informed me that the Spanish Government had delayed for a considerable time to transmit to Onís the final instructions by virtue of which the treaty [with the United States] was concluded, and which had been prepared by Yrujo's predecessor. The determination was taken only after the failure of obtaining at Aix la Chapelle the mediation of the allied powers with the colonies, under a feeling of irritation against Great Britain as the author of the failure, and from a conviction that any attempt to subjugate [the colonies] by force was hopeless whilst the danger of a rupture with the United States continued to exist.

Literally construed, the explanation reported by Gallatin was not correct, for the Congress of Aix-la-Chapelle was still in session when Irujo sent Onís the instructions of October 10, 1818, under which he negotiated the treaty with Adams. Nevertheless, the adverse decision of the Congress on the intervention desired by Spain was made a foregone conclusion by the very strong letter written to the British ambassador at Madrid by Castlereagh on September 1, 1818, as he was on the point of setting out for Aix-la-Chapelle. Although this was a private letter, the substance of it was clearly intended to be communicated to the Spanish court. Consequently, while the question requires further study, it seems probable that Spain surrendered to the United States partly because her hopes of an intervention by the powers assembled at Aix-la-Chapelle had been blasted; and the episode provides one more illustration of the intimate triangular relationship that existed between the affairs of Europe, Latin America, and the United States in the period of the present study.

The immediate result was a resounding diplomatic victory for the United States. Adams recorded it in his diary with deep satisfaction and with reverent though slightly puzzled gratitude to the "all-beneficent Disposer of events" who had "brought it about in a manner utterly unexpected and by means the most extraordinary and unforeseen." It was certainly a highly important treaty, for, aside from the fact that it settled many vexatious problems, it greatly strengthened the position of the United States in the Gulf of Mexico and gave it its first treaty claim to territory on the Pacific coast. This "Transcontinental Treaty," as it has been appropriately named, marked one of the principal stages in the territorial expansion of the United States and in its rise to world power.

Nevertheless, the treaty had some most unfortunate repercussions in the field of Latin American relations. The surrender of the United States' claim to Texas provoked sharp criticism at home and gave rise almost at once to a demand for the reannexation of Texas. Coinciding with the establishment of Mexican Independence, this demand clouded the relations of the United States with its new neighbor to the south from the very beginning of its national existence, and set in motion a train of events that by the end of the next generation had antagonized Spanish Americans everywhere against the United States.

More immediately unfortunate was the resentment that the very negotiation of the treaty aroused against the United States in Spanish America. This resentment arose from the belief that the United States had deliberately sacrificed the Spanish American cause in order to further its own national interests. In its extreme form this belief was based on the assumption that the treaty contained a secret clause by which, as a part of the price that it paid Spain for Florida, the United States had obligated itself not to recognize or otherwise aid the Spanish American revolutionists. In its milder form, the belief was based on the conviction that, whatever the intention of the United States might have been, its settlement of its difficulties with Spain made it possible for the latter to concentrate all her energies on the subjugation of her colonies.

In one form or another, this belief was widespread in Europe and America. In May 1819 Gallatin reported that it was held in usually well informed quarters in Paris; and a month earlier the American vice-consul at Buenos Aires, W. G. Miller, listed it as one of the chief reasons for the rapidly rising resentment of the people of that city against the United States.

"We are no longer looked up to [by the people of Buenos Aires] as Americans, the protectors of liberty and the supporters of the independence and of the cause of our South American brothers [concluded Miller], but rather as *neutrals* determined to assist Spain in the reconquest of the country.

The flames of resentment were fanned by British rivals of the United States; for example, the Buenos Aires government was told by its London agents, Hullett Brothers, that the treaty was a betrayal of the Spanish American cause.

There can be no doubt that the treaty would have injured that cause if the Spanish government had been able to take advantage of the opportunity afforded by it; but it would be difficult to sustain the further charge that the United States deliberately sacrificed the interests of Spanish America to its own. For one thing, there was no truth whatever in the charge that the United States had obligated itself, by a secret article or otherwise, not to recognize the independence of the new Spanish American states. Indeed, its refusal to make any commitment to that effect was one of the main reasons for Spain's long delay in ratifying the treaty, the ratifications of which were not exchanged until February 22, 1821, precisely two years after Adams and Onís signed it.

Again, there appears to be no foundation for the assertion, which has been repeated by historians in the United States itself, that the American government postponed recognition of Spanish American independence until the treaty had been safely negotiated and ratified. Statements made by Adams himself can be cited in support of this view, but they must be discounted heavily, for they were obviously made for political and diplomatic effect, to appease the unrecognized governments of Spanish America and their impatient champions in Congress.

The fact is that, as the present chapter and the two preceding chapters should have made abundantly clear, the policy which delayed recognition had been decided upon long before the beginning of Adams's negotiation with Onís and was based upon considerations which had little if anything to do with it: and it is not easy to see how recognition could have been hastened appreciably even if there had never been a Spanish negotiation. After the negotiation was completed by the exchange of ratifications at Washington (February 22, 1821) more than a year elapsed before President Monroe sent the message to Congress that committed his administration to recognition. It would seem, therefore, that in the long story of the cautious, tentative, intermittent advance of the United States towards the recognition of the new states, the retarding influence of the Spanish negotiation was relatively unimportant.

The postponement of recognition was mainly due to two other factors: first, to the situation in Spanish America, where there was no government that was clearly entitled to recognition; and second, to the attitude of Europe, which, the administration believed, made it dangerous to recognize any Spanish American government, no matter how meritorious its case might be. Until the latter part of

1818 both factors remained fairly constant and both were adverse to recognition. Then they became somewhat more favorable as a result of the stand taken by England at Aix-la-Chapelle, the progress of the revolution in South America, and the good impression created by DeForest's mission. The administration at Washington promptly made unmistakable though cautious preparations to abandon its policy of watchful waiting and begin its recognition of Spanish American independence.

It is important to note, however, that these preparations contemplated recognition by the concerted action of the United States and Great Britain, as proposed in Adams's instructions to Rush of January 1819. There is no good reason to believe that the administration was ready to brave the hazards of recognition alone; and when Castlereagh again, as in 1818, turned a cold shoulder to the invitation to concerted action, the rebuff was only another warning to Washington to make haste slowly along the road to recognition. Progress was not renewed again until nearly three years later, under profoundly different circumstances.

4 FROM *Bradford Perkins*
Castlereagh and Adams: England and the
United States, 1812–1823

The outbreak of revolution in South America had served the interests of the United States in the negotiations over Florida. However, the revolutions in Spain, Italy, and Greece in the 1820s created new dilemmas for Washington. France intervened in Spain to restore Ferdinand VII to the throne. This raised the question in the minds of many whether she would also assist her neighbor to recover her lost provinces in the Western Hemisphere. Further, in 1823 Russia issued a ukase, warning foreign vessels not to come within 100 Italian miles of the Alaska coast down to the 51st parallel. The latter line extended well into the Oregon country and posed a challenge which could not be ignored.

Canning, the British Foreign Secretary, shared America's concern over the turn of events in Europe and America, and he proposed that Washington and London issue a joint manifesto designed to prevent future European intervention in the Western Hemisphere. While this was an idea which commended itself to even Madison and Jefferson, it was opposed by Adams whose distrust of Canning and Britain dated back to the War of 1812. Therefore Monroe decided to issue a unilateral declaration which joined a confirmation of the United States' determination to stay out of European affairs with a ringing declaration that America would firmly oppose further colonization in the Western Hemisphere by the nations of Europe. The intricacies of the diplomacy leading to the Monroe Doctrine and the importance of the declaration are examined in Bradford Perkins, Castlereagh and Adams.

THE MONROE DOCTRINE

Rush reported his exchanges with Canning in two sets of dispatches. The first, describing their correspondence but not the discouraging interviews following the Foreign Secretary's return to London, reached Washington on October 9, 1823, the very day Polignac approved in principle the memorandum Canning thrust upon him. Adams was still rattling across Pennsylvania on his return from Massachusetts, where he had visited his lonely father, a

SOURCE. Bradford Perkins, *Castlereagh and Adams: England and the United States, 1812–1823* (Berkeley and Los Angeles: University of California Press, 1964), pp. 326–347. Reprinted by permission of the Regents of the University of California and the author.

widower since 1818. President Monroe, who only awaited Adams' return before taking a short vacation of his own, interrupted preparations to scan the dispatches.

James Monroe and those he consulted agreed that Canning's offer posed "the most momentous [question] which has ever been offered . . . since that of Independence." In the early years of the republic European powers usually called the tune. The War of 1812 showed America's impatience with passive defense, while the Treaty of Ghent and Castlereagh's postwar policy revealed a growing, somewhat grudging British recognition of her power. Now Canning offered a limited alliance, an understanding nominally between equals, really an entente on British principles. Should the United States accept? The isolationist spirit, the almost universal conviction that America and Europe occupied distinct spheres, urged refusal. Yet during the Revolution, the undeclared war with France, and the Louisiana crisis, the Americans sought foreign assistance. Had Castlereagh's policy unintentionally taught them to value their own worth? Had they now the confidence to strike out on their own?

The President first turned to his old mentors, Jefferson and Madison. Forwarding the correspondence to them, Monroe stated his opinion that Britain at last found herself forced to choose between autocracy and constitutionalism, that if the Europeans succeeded in Latin America they would attack the United States, and that "we had better meet the proposition fully, & decisively," thus encouraging her to serve "in a cause which tho' important to her, as to balance of power, commerce &c, is vital to us, as to government." The President did not explicitly recommend acceptance of Canning's five points.

Thomas Jefferson and James Madison advised Monroe to accept Canning's offer even though it meant, as Jefferson pointed out, postponing Cuban ambitions. "Great Britain is the nation which can do us the most harm of any one, or all on earth, " Jefferson wrote; "and with her on our side we need not fear the whole world." The separation of Europe and America would be assured. More specifically the two Virginians, ignoring gaps in Canning's proposal, expected current threats to collapse in the face of Anglo-American union. "Whilst it must ensure success, in the event of an appeal to force," Madison predicted, "it doubles the chance of success without that appeal." For the moment Monroe kept this advice secret, even from Adams.

The President, who returned to Washington on November 4, convened his cabinet on the afternoon of the seventh. Five men—Monroe, Adams, Secretary of War Calhoun, Secretary of the Navy Southard, and Attorney General Wirt—settled the reply to Britain, an important declaration to Russia, and Monroe's message at the opening of Congress on December 2. William Wirt and Samuel Southard, old friends of the President's, contributed little to the first meeting or the half dozen that followed. On Latin America, the most debated question, Calhoun spoke the language of caution and his elder, Adams, the language of bold independence. The President heard all views, at times inclined toward Calhoun's, and ultimately backed Adams'.

Until November 21, when Monroe read a preliminary version of his message, none of the secretaries expected the President to make a general declaration of principles in his message to Congress. As was then customary, each secretary prepared a few paragraphs on his department for the President's guidance. Adams' suggestions, submitted on November 13, ignored the Latin-American question, the Secretary expecting to handle this in diplomatic correspondence. His draft concentrated on the Pacific Coast. The ukase, Adams observed, had led to discussions in which the American government asserted that "the American Continents by the free and independent condition which they have assumed and maintain, are henceforth not to be considered as subjects for future Colonization by any European Power." The President accepted this passage almost verbatim.

As a maxim the noncolonization doctrine, a less acid expression of the views of Adams inflicted on Stratford Canning in their worst quarrel, challenged England more than any other power. Yet although the Secretary sometimes considered it applicable to British claims in the Oregon country, the doctrine never played a major part in that dispute, nor did it have relevance to current British ambitions. Noncolonization was laid down at this time solely because of the Russian ukase.

When Monroe read his draft Adams, happy to hear the paragraph on colonization, took exception to another presidential passage. The Chief Executive cast a benevolent eye upon the Greeks, then struggling to cast off their Turkish yoke, and spoke "in terms of the most pointed reprobation of the late invasion of Spain by France, and of the princples upon which it was undertaken by the open avowal of the King of France." Like many Republicans at the opening of the French Revolution and many contemporaries as well, the President allowed enthusiasm for self-government and dislike of tyranny to undermine his devotion to isolation. A strong anti-monarchist, an even stronger isolationist, Adams protested that Monroe's proposed statement, by breaking down the idea of two spheres, weakened the noncolonization doctrine and objections to European projects in the Western Hemisphere. The statement might even involve the country in serious controversy over non-American issues.

The President apparently felt the force of Adams' arguments. Despite Calhoun's contrary opinions he altered his plans. After expressing sympathy for Spain the message delivered to Congress added, "In the wars of the European powers, in matters relating to themselves, we have never taken any part, nor does it comport with our policy, so to do." Monroe thus made explicit the traditional isolationism of his people, a feeling as old as and more realistic than their prorepublicanism. This became the second tenet of the doctrine bearing his name. The third required much more discussion.

When the President returned to Washington Adams showed him a note delivered on October 16 by Baron Tuyll, the Russian minister. Tuyll announced and justified Russia's adamant refusal to recognize the rebellious colonies. He also praised the American decision to remain neutral even after recognition. This warning against American aid to Latin America, if indeed it was a warning, was temperate enough to permit Adams to reply, for the President, with a mild defense of recognition and a hope that Russia too would remain neutral. Otherwise the United States might reconsider its own neutrality. . . .

Statements to the world through Tuyll and Congress made it plain that the American government intended to act as an independent power rather than as a British satellite. They did not make a reply to Canning less necessary. Unwillingness to act as "a cock-boat in the wake of a British man-of-war," in other words, made it certain Canning's plan would not gain unconditional, immediate approval, but did not disbar negotiations on the basis of that plan.

Adams' diary pictures the President as uncertain of the proper reply to England, not as inclined to accept Canning's offer. Even Calhoun, the most alarmed member of the inner circle, proposed to give Rush only discretionary authority to accept the offer in an emergency. All apparently agreed to seek modifications if time permitted, particularly to request or require British recognition of Latin states. At one point the President endorsed Calhoun's suggestion. Adams rather easily talked him out of this idea, and in the end the President adopted Adams' sterner position.

Instructions to Rush, revised several times as the President edged toward decision, 'bore date of November 29, a few days after Monroe had completed his forthcoming address. At Monroe's direction Adams struck out an explicit statement that until Britain granted recognition "we can see no foundation upon which the concurrent action of the two Governments can be harmonized." The instructions made the point in more diplomatic language. Only if Britain extended recognition was Rush authorized to move "in concert" with her. This last clause, whatever courses it approved, clearly did not mean joint action along the lines Canning originally proposed, even should the Foreign Secretary bring his colleagues around to recognition. Monroe and Adams promised to consider joint as opposed to parallel action only if, a new emergency arising, Rush referred home further proposals.

Adams, who never claimed credit for rejecting the British offer (he took pride chiefly in the noncolonization doctrine), stood nearer his colleagues than is often said. No one desired unconditional approval. In his first comments on Canning's offer the President merely said that his inclination was to "meet" it, not that he favored the joint manifesto Canning urged. Obviously the President wished to widen the breach between Britain and the allies and to protect Latin America. He believed the reply to Tuyll and the message to Congress did so. "We certainly meet, in full extent, the proposition of M^r. Canning," he wrote Jefferson. "With G. Britain, we have, it is presumed, acted fairly & fully to all her objects, & have a right to expect, a corresponding conduct on her part," he wrote his immediate predecessor. Forwarding the President's message to Rush, Adams observed, "The concurrence of these sentiments with those of the British Government as exhibited in the proposals of Mr. Canning, will be obvious to you. It will now remain for Great Britain to make hers equally public. The moral effect upon the councils of the Allies, to deter them from any interposition of force between Spain and America, will be complete." The form might differ from Canning's scheme. The effect did not, President and Secretary both believed.

On December 2, 1823, instructions having gone to Rush and a reply to Tuyll, Congress heard the President's message. Three of fifty-one paragraphs dealt with foreign affairs, an early one stating the noncolonization doctrine and two later ones mingling isolationist sentiments and warnings against intervention by Europe.

Not for thirty years did Americans name these three paragraphs the Monroe Doctrine. From the beginning, however, they valued the principles laid down by the last of the Virginia dynasty. Within a week Adams noted that the nation universally approved the message. The British chargé agreed. "The explicit and manly tone," he informed Canning a month later, "has evidently found in every bosom a chord which vibrates in strict unison with the sentiments so conveyed. They have been echoed from one end of the union to the other." Monroe's decision to ignore the advice of his two neighbors and predecessors, to strike out boldly and independently with a declaration of principle despite possible risks, drew support throughout the nation.

Just after the message Washington received a rumor, in fact unfounded, that 12,000 French troops were about to sail for South America. This alarmed editors Niles and Gales as well as the President, who talked briefly of the need to "unite with the British Govt, in measures, to prevent the interference of the allied powers." Monroe soon cooled, perhaps under Adams' influence. New instructions to Rush, carried by a secret agent to Europe to ferret out allied plans, spoke only of a "concert of operations" and studiously avoided any mention of joint action.

In a few days a dispatch arrived from Daniel Sheldon, the chargé at Paris. Sheldon reported that, neither the Bourbon monarchy scheme nor any other having come to a focus, the United States need not fear an immediate descent on Latin America. A second dispatch two weeks later repeated this prediction. The scare passed. In the spring Henry Clay withdrew a resolution endorsing the nonintervention doctrine, saying, "Events and circumstances, subsequent to the communication of the Message, evinced, that if such a purpose were ever seriously entertained, it had been relinquished."

Monroe's message, aimed partly at Latin America, had no clear effect there. The leader of the fight for liberty, Simón Bolívar, completely ignored it in his correspondence. Most South American leaders continued to regard England as their chief defense against European intervention.

Europeans, who also felt that the message scarcely altered the practical situation, nevertheless reacted strongly to the President's

sentiments. Liberals contrasted Monroe's enlightened views with
those of their own governments. The dominant groups denounced
his presumption. The noncolonization doctrine challenged international law; the warning against intervention denied legitimist ambitions; the prorepublican theme threatened traditional
European doctrines. The United States, Prince Metternich complained, "have suddenly left a sphere too narrow for their ambition,
and have astonished Europe by a new act of revolt, more unpro-
voked, fully as audacious, and no less dangerous than the former.
. . . If this flood of evil doctrines . . . should extend over the whole
of America, what would become of . . . that conservative system
which has saved Europe from complete dissolution?"

In Britain praise outweighed criticism. The message reached
Falmouth by government packet on December 24 and passed to all
the kingdom. The *Caledonian Mercury*, usually friendly to the United
States, scoffed at Monroe's "obscure innuendos." Other papers
gave the message the attention it deserved, the *Chronicle* pronounc-
ing it "worthy of the occasion and the people, who seem destined
to occupy so large a space in the future history of the world." No
editor denounced the republican cast which so upset Metternich.
All withheld comment on the isolationist passages, apparently
considering them mere truisms. The papers concentrated upon
the noncolonization and nonintervention doctrines.

Several editors objected to the former, a "startling general
principle," a "curious idea," a "grave and somewhat novel
doctrine." The *Star*, most critical of the entire message, declared:
"The plain *Yankee* of the matter is, that the United States wish to
monopolize to themselves the privilege of colonising . . . every . . .
part of the American Continent." In the Oregon country and elsewhere Britain must not accept this proposition. Not one British
voice defended Monroe, but many papers passed over noncolonization in silence.

Britons regarded the nonintervention doctrine as the heart of the
message, and on the whole they liked it. Even the *Star*, which considered Monroe hypocritical "to place on the basis of a bounden
duty, what is, in plain truth, a matter of the sheerest self-interest,"
welcomed his reinforcement of British efforts. "The President has
made just such a declaration . . . as it is to the interest of this
country that he should have made," opined the *Herald*. "This is
plain speaking, and it is just speaking," pontificated the *Times*.
Both the *Times* and the *Chronicle* contrasted America's boldness with

the British government's alleged lack of courage. The latter paper even maintained that an English declaration as forthright as Monroe's would have prevented the French invasion of Spain which began the whole crisis.

The *Courier*, once bitterly anti-Yankee and long a mouthpiece of British conservatism, capped British comment. "The question of the Independence and recognition of the South American States, may now be considered as at rest," the paper declared. Europe would no longer dare to plan action against the former Spanish colonies. "Protected by the two nations that possess the institutions, and speak the language of freedom—by Great Britain on one side, and by the United States on the other, their independence is placed beyond the reach of danger." On the great issue of the day England and the United States stood together as allies for freedom.

Canning reacted less favorably to the message and the decision, unknown to the public but to him painful, to refuse the offer of joint action. Six months earlier his cousin's overoptimistic reports led to dreams of a virtual alliance, an agreement far transcending a joint statement on Latin America. In October, after discussing general negotiations with Rush and Stratford Canning, he turned to his cousin, who remained in the office, and said "he should be inclined to take this opportunity to make a clearance of all American questions." The collapse of hopes for an entente on Latin America destroyed Canning's interest in other negotiations. Rush's conversations with Stratford Canning and Huskisson dwindled slowly into nothing during the first half of 1824. Canning made little effort to stir the negotiations into life.

Nor did the Foreign Secretary show interest when Rush read Adams' instructions of November 29, laying down terms on which coöperation might develop. With the Latin-American problem anesthetized by the Polignac memorandum, Canning saw no need for a joint statement, particularly one quite different from his original proposal, and felt free to take up new questions posed by Monroe's message.

Canning particularly objected to the noncolonization doctrine. He complained so strongly that Rush quickly dropped the matter. Canning drew up but wisely did not deliver an argumentative note in which he compared Alexander's ukase with "the new doctrine of the President," concluding that "we cannot yield obedience to either." Later, in instructions to Stratford Canning and Huskisson, he declared the British government "prepared to reject [Monroe's principle] in the most unequivocal manner, maintaining that whatever right of colonizing the unappropriated parts of America had been hitherto enjoyed . . . may still be exercised in perfect freedom, and without affording the slightest cause of umbrage to the United States."

Although Canning saw advantages in acting hand in hand with the United States he shrank from appearing at St. Petersburg with a power avowing principles so different. He also did not like or even profess to understand the American proposal to limit permanent British settlements to the area between 51° and 55°, and when the American minister presented this plan Canning replied, "Heyday! What is here? Do I read Mr Rush's meaning aright?" Consequently he ordered his ambassador in Russia to negotiate separately. No harm resulted. Russia abandoned her claim to broad maritime jurisdiction and, by separate agreements with her two adversaries, abandoned the Oregon country.

George Canning considered the nonintervention doctrine in some ways useful to England. He even professed unconcern at the refusal to act jointly. After Polignac he did not fear an allied descent upon South America. He counted on Monroe's message to give pause to planners of a European congress on Latin-American affairs. "The Congress was broken in all its limits before, but the President's speech gives it the *coup de grace*," he felt, overoptimistically as events proved. "The effect of the ultra-Liberalism of our Yankee cooperators, on the ultra-despotism of our Aix la Chapelle allies, gives me just the balance that I wanted," he informed his friend Bagot.

In more important ways the presidential announcement unsettled Canning. A proud and practical politician, he disliked having Monroe steal a march on him. "Are you not," Lord Grey asked Holland, "delighted with the American speech? What a contrast to the conduct . . . of our Government. . . . Canning will have the glory of following in the wake of the President of the United States." Canning did not like to have his enemies free to speak this way, particularly since he believed, and said Rush agreed, that "his Govᵗ. would *not* have spoken out, but for what passed between us." Canning felt Monroe had tricked and defeated him.

More than mere pique upset the Foreign Secretary. Canning did not want close economic and political ties between the United States and South America, partly because these might lead to discrimination against English commerce and partly because Britain, already at odds with Europe, would find herself isolated. The Foreign Secretary still hoped for negotiations between Spain and the Latin Americans, a course Monroe clearly disapproved. Because Canning, in the words of an admiring biographer, considered "constitutional monarchy . . . the true *via media* between democracy and despotism," he hoped to keep monarchist ideas alive in South America. Monroe's message was a paean on popular government. Canning felt he must regain the lead from one who blew "a blast on the republican trumpet, while sheltered behind the shield of England."

The Polignac memorandum, circulated to European diplomats shortly after its signature and sent by Canning to Rush a few weeks later, remained secret from the public until 1824. At the opening of Parliament in February, Canning, assailed for following a less decisive tack than Monroe, defended ministers with a paraphrase. On March 4 he presented the memorandum, still with deletions, to the House of Commons, and government spokesmen exploited it. Lord Liverpool asked if such a *démarche*, which the French had been forced to accept, was not "worth a thousand official declarations." The government also revealed its refusal to attend a congress on Latin America, a proposal reluctantly made by Ferdinand. These actions showed Europe and Latin America, neither of whom needed much convincing, that Britain still posed the most effective barrier to outside interference in the imperial war.

Fostering monarchical principles in Latin America proved more difficult, even impossible. After the downfall of Iturbide in Mexico they virtually disappeared. Moreover King Ferdinand, obdurate as ever, refused to countenance negotiations with his erstwhile subjects, and continued presence of French troops in Spain angered Canning. Supported by Liverpool he decided to challenge the cabinet majority.

In August, 1824, Canning forced agreement to recognize Buenos Aires, although George IV objected that "the whole proceedings . . . are premature"—at a time when, except in Peru, Spain had no armies on the mainland. On the last day of the year, after a lengthy battle during which Canning threatened to resign, the Foreign Secretary won cabinet approval of a note to Spain announcing England's intention to recognize Buenos Aires, Mexico, and Colombia. The King again objected to his ministers' precipitancy —"I have already expressed my wishes . . . & wishes when coming from the King are always to be considered & understood as

Commands"—but recognition proceeded as Canning and Liverpool planned. A year and a half after Canning first approached Rush the British and American governments were aligned. They were also rivals for Latin-American favor and commerce.

Canning's efforts to counteract the nonintervention doctrine, usually carried out with a tact belying his reputation, failed to pull the wool over Richard Rush's hypercritical eyes. Late in 1824 he wrote: "It would be an entire mistake to suppose, that because of the partial and guarded approach to us by Britain last year, on the south American question, she feels any increase of good will towards us."

Most Americans disagreed, and in 1824 and 1825 Anglo-American friendship reached unprecedented levels. Early in 1824 an alliance on Latin-American questions gained wide support although, as Addington reported, it could be "attributed as much to the hope of acquiring additional security to their own institutions as from any inherent affection for Great Britain, or disinterested ardour in the cause of transatlantic Liberty." Alliance talk died with the collapse of threats to Latin-America; friendship did not. The tariff debate of 1824 totally lacked the anti-British emphasis of that of 1816. At a White House reception the President, speaking in a tone to be overheard, praised British policy and welcomed the growth of Anglo-American concord.

In the spring of 1825, learning of Charles Vaughan's appointment as minister to the United States, Addington requested a leave to escape the oppressive Washington heat. He looked back upon his tenure with satisfaction. "It is scarcely possible that a man should arrive under better auspices than Vaughan," he reported, "for 2/3ds of the Americans are just now well-disposed towards us, and Clay [the former war hawk now secretary of state] says that he is quite in love with Mr Canning." An honest man well aware that outstanding issues or new ones could spoil the scene, Addington added: "How long this may last I do not pretend to conjecture."

Addington's ease paid tribute to George Canning and perhaps even more to Lord Castlereagh, for Canning reaped where Castlereagh had sown. From the spring of 1814 onward, at first slowly and almost inadvertently, British policy moved toward conciliation. The Rush–Bagot agreement and the convention of 1818 were positive sides of this policy. Probably more important, Castlereagh and then Canning sought to stifle controversy before it became serious or, better, to avoid it altogether. "Let us hasten settlement, if we can; but let us postpone the day of difference, if it must come; which however I trust it need not," Canning wrote. This policy had the disadvantage of leaving issues like Oregon and West Indian trade for future dispute. In the immediate sense it paid impressive dividends.

Even Rush, hostile and suspicious, admitted, "Mine have been plain-sailing times," and in general the American political world praised England for muffling winds of controversy. An observant British traveler, no mere panegyrist of the United States, wrote in 1823 that "there are few, whose good opinion is worth having, who do not unite in good will towards the people of my native country." This much had the climate changed since 1812.

In the Liverpool speech which charmed Christopher Hughes, George Canning "express[ed] the gratification which he felt, in common with the great mass of the intelligent and liberal men of both countries, to see the animosities necessarily attendant on a state of hostility so rapidly wearing away." He welcomed the growth of friendship between "two nations united by a common language, a common spirit of commercial enterprise, and a common regard for well-regulated liberty." Appropriately, Canning did not mention contrary factors—the continuing British air of superiority, American touchiness and ambition, commercial rivalry, England's distrust of republicanism, and America's of monarchy. Still he fairly described a process taking place on both sides of the Atlantic.

Basically the new relationship reflected the growth of American power and stability and of Britain's sometimes half-reluctant recognition of this growth. America has "already taken her rank among the first powers of Christendom," the *Annual Register* observed in the volume for 1824. Few Englishmen yet placed the United States on a par with their own country. They did see that the American form of government "has survived the tender period of infancy, and outlived the prophecies of its downfall. . . . It has been found serviceable both in peace and war, and may well claim from the nation it has saved . . . the votive benediction of 'Esto perpetua.'" Perpetual or not—Calhoun and Jefferson Davis would speak to that—the union had gained a position beyond foreign challenge. Capable and bold diplomacy followed a dangerous and ill-fought war. The new American generation vindicated the aspirations of their fathers in 1776.

SUGGESTED FURTHER READING

The Challenge of Neutrality
The Coming of War
Peace and the Postwar Settlement

THE CHALLENGE OF
NEUTRALITY

A favorable account of Washington's foreign policy is to be found in
L. M. Sears, *George Washington and the French Revolution* (Detroit, 1960).
Felix Gilbert, *To the Farewell Address* (Princeton, 1961) skillfully examines
events leading to Washington's statement and analyzes the role Hamilton
had in drafting it. The standard account of Jay's Treaty is to be found in
S. F. Bemis, *Jay's Treaty* (New York, 1925). The severe criticism of Hamilton
in Bemis' work is modified in A. L. Burt, *The United States, Great Britain and
British North America* (New Haven, 1940). A more recent study is Bradford
Perkins, *The First Rapprochment: England and the United States, 1795–1805*
(Philadelphia, 1955). A cool and balanced examination of the period is to
be found in Paul A. Varg, *Foreign Policies of the Founding Fathers* (East Lansing,
1963). Two admirable books by J. C. Miller, *The Federalist Era, 1789–1801*
(New York, 1960) and *Alexander Hamilton: Portrait in Paradox* (New York,
(Durham, N.C., 1958) and *The Quasi-War: The Politics and Diplomacy of the
Undeveloped War with France, 1797–1801* (New York, 1966). The history of
John Adams (Philadelphia, 1957). The most recent and balanced examinations of foreign policy are in Alexander DeConde, *The Entangling Alliance*
1953), examine both the general period and the specific role played in it by
Hamilton. The Presidency of John Adams can most fruitfully be studied by
a reading of Gilbert Chinard, *Honest John Adams* (Boston, 1933) and Page
Smith, *John Adams* (New York, 1962). See also S. G. Kurtz, *The Presidency of*
the Louisiana Purchase is told succinctly in A. B. Darling, *Our Rising Empire
1763–1803* (New Haven, 1940). For a detailed examination of the western
aspects of this issue, see A. P. Whitaker, *The Mississippi Question, 1795–1803*
(New York, 1934). Additional material may be found in E. W. Lyons, *The
Louisiana Purchase in French Diplomacy, 1759–1804* (Norman, Oklahoma,
1934) and George Dangerfield, *Chancellor Robert R. Livingston of New York,
1746–1813* (New York, 1960). A refreshing and informative study of

Jefferson's relationship with France is L. S. Kaplan, *Jefferson and France* (New Haven, 1966). Articles of particular interest include S. F. Bemis, "Washington's Farewell Address: A Foreign Policy of Independence," *Amer. Hist. Rev.*, XXXIX (1934), 250–268; Alexander DeConde, "Washington's Farewell Address, the French Alliance, and the Election of 1796." *Miss. Valley Hist. Rev.*, XLIII, (1957), 641–658; Joseph Charles, "The Jay Treaty: The Origins of the American Party System," *William and Mary Quarterly*, XII, 3rd ser. (1953), 581–630.

THE COMING OF WAR

The most judicious and balanced account of neutral rights is to be found in A. L. Burt, *The United States, Great Britain and British North America* (New Haven, 1940). Further material on the problems on maritime issues may be examined in W. H. Phillips and A. H. Reede, *Neutrality* (New York, 1936) and E. F. Hecksher, *The Continental System* (Oxford, 1922). The embargo and its consequences are fully examined in L. M. Sears, *Jefferson and the Embargo* (Durham, N.C., 1927) and W. W. Jennings, *The American Embargo, 1807–1809* (Iowa City, 1921). The classic histories of the War of 1812 are Henry Adams, *History of the United States of America during the Administrations of Jefferson and Madison*, 9 vols. (New York, 1891) and A. T. Mahan, *Sea Power and the War of 1812*, 2 vols. (Boston, 1905). J. W. Pratt, *Expansionists of 1812* (New York, 1925) is the standard account of the role of the West in bringing on the war. Bradford Perkins, *Prologue to War* (Berkeley, 1961) is one of the most recent and fullest studies of the war. He examines maritime and political issues and is critical of the leadership provided in this period by Jefferson and Madison. Reginald Horsman, *Causes of the War of 1812* (Philadelphia, 1962) is a balanced analysis of the war which stresses the European origins of the issues which bring on the conflict. Roger Brown, *The Republic in Peril* (New York, 1964) argues that party conflict and division was a more significant factor in explaining attitudes toward the war than has been commonly supposed. Irving Brant, *James Madison: The President, 1809–1812* (Indianapolis, 1956) suggests, not wholly convincingly, that President Madison's abilities as a leader have been underestimated. Patrick C. T. White, *A Nation on Trial: America and the War of 1812* (New York, 1965) examines the maritime and domestic issues and suggests that the war came largely because of the challenge to American sovereignty. A general and popular account of the war is A. Z. Carr, *The Coming of the War* (New York, 1960). One of the best biographies of a leading advocate of the war is Bernard Mayo, *Henry Clay* (Boston, 1937). An excellent summary of various interpretations of the war may be found in W. H. Goodman, "The Origins of the War of 1812: A Survey of Changing Interpretations," *Miss. Valley Hist. Rev.*, XXVIII

(1941), 171–186. An informative and useful study of the effects of British policies on the South and West is G. R. Taylor, "Agrarian Discontent in the Mississippi Valley Preceding the War of 1812," *Journal of Political Economy*, XXXIX (1931), 471–505. N. K. Risjord, "1812 : Conservatives, War Hawks, and the Nation's Honor," *William and Mary Quarterly*, XVIII (1961), 196–210, is an admirable study which suggests that the desire to preserve the nation's honor was a crucial factor in leading to the declaration of war. Other articles of value include Margaret K. Latimer, "South Carolina—a Protagonist of the War of 1812," *Amer. Hist. Rev.*, LXI, (1956), 914–929; Abbot Smith, "Mr Madison's War: An Unsuccessful Experiment in the Conduct of National Policy," *Political Science Quarterly*, LVII (1942), 229–246; Reginald Horsman, "Western War Aims, 1811–1812," *Insana Magazine of History*, LIII (1957), 1–18, and "British Indian Policy in the Northwest, 1807–1812," *Miss. Valley Hist.*, XIV (1958), 51–66; and L. M. Hacker, "Western Land Hunger and the War of 1812," *Miss. Valley Hist. Rev.*, X (1924), 365–395.

PEACE AND THE POSTWAR
SETTLEMENT

The standard accounts of the negotiations leading to the Treaty of Ghent are A. T. Mahan, *Sea Power in its Relation to the War of 1812*, 2 vols. (Boston, 1905) and Henry Adams, *History of the United States during the Administrations of Jefferson and Madison*, 9 vols. (New York, 1891). The fullest treatment is in F. A. Updyke, *The Diplomacy of the War of 1812* (Baltimore, 1915). The most recent and extensive examination of the period is Bradford Perkins, *Castlereagh and Adams: England and the United States, 1812–1823* (Berkeley and Los Angeles, 1964). More concise examinations of the making of the peace are in Patrick C. T. White, *A Nation on Trial: America and the War of 1812* (New York, 1965) and A. L. Burt, *The United States, Great Britain and British North America* (New Haven, 1940). An excellent account of the peace negotiations is to be found in George Dangerfield, *The Era of Good Feelings* (London, 1953). A popular account which stresses the ability of the American diplomats is F. L. Engleman, *The Peace of Christmas Eve* (New York, 1962). Irving Brant, *James Madison: Commander in Chief, 1812–1836* (Indianapolis, 1961) portrays the President as an effective war leader who guided his nation to a final victory. Raymond Walters, *Albert Gallatin: Jeffersonian Financier and Diplomat* (New York, 1957) is a balanced and careful account of the negotiations and Gallatin's contribution to them. See also J. H. Powell, *Richard Rush, Republican Diplomat, 1780–1859* (Philadelphia, 1942). The Convention of 1818 is examined in full detail in A. L. Burt, *The United States, Great Britain and British North America* (New Haven, 1940) and S. F. Bemis, *John Quincy Adams and the Foundation of American Foreign Policy* (New York, 1949). A. P. Whitaker, *The United States and the Independence of Latin America* (Baltimore, 1941), C. C. Griffin, *The United States and the Disruption of the Spanish Empire, 1810–1823* (New York, 1933), and P. C. Brooks, *Diplomacy and the Borderlands: The Adams–Onís Treaty of 1819* (Berkeley, 1933) cover in detail the problems of the Floridas.

The standard mongraphs on the Monroe Doctrine are Dexter Perkins, *The Monroe Doctrine 1823–1826* (Cambridge, 1927) and *A History of the Monroe Doctrine* (Boston, 1955). Bradford Perkins, *Castlereagh and Adams: England the United States, 1812–1823* (Berkeley and Los Angeles, 1964) modifies some of the findings in these earlier studies. Details of particular issues may be found in J. A. Logan, Jr., *No Transfer* (New Haven, 1961) and J. F. Rippy, *Rivalry of the United States and Great Britain over Latin America, 1808–1830* (Baltimore, 1923).